Wicca Book of Spells:

A New Book of Shadows for Modern Witchcraft

[by Luna Lovegood]

Wicca Book of Spells - Copyright © 2019 by Luna Lovegood

Legal & Disclaimer

The information contained in this book and its contents is not designed to replace or take the place of any form of medical or professional advice; and is not meant to replace the need for independent medical, financial, legal or other professional advice or services, as may be required. The content and information in this book has been provided for educational and entertainment purposes only.

The content and information contained in this book have been compiled from sources deemed reliable, and it is accurate to the best of the Author's knowledge, information and belief. However, the Author cannot guarantee its accuracy and validity and cannot be held liable for any errors and/or omissions. Further, changes are periodically made to this book as and when needed. Where appropriate and/or necessary, you must consult a professional (including but not limited to your doctor, attorney, financial advisor or such other professional advisor) before using any of the suggested remedies, techniques, or information in this book.

Upon using the contents and information contained in this book, you agree to hold harmless the Author from and against any damages, costs, and expenses, including any legal fees potentially resulting from the application of any of the information provided by this book. This disclaimer applies to any loss, damages or injury caused by the use and application, whether directly or indirectly, of any advice or information presented, whether for breach of contract, tort, negligence, personal injury, criminal intent, or under any other cause of action.

You agree to accept all risks of using the information presented inside this book.

You agree that by continuing to read this book, where appropriate and/or necessary, you shall consult a professional (including but not limited to your doctor, attorney, or financial advisor or such other advisor as needed) before using any of the suggested remedies, techniques, or information in this book.

Table of Contents

Introduction

The word Wicca originates from the Old English and means simply, "witch". Older Germanic languages attribute additional meanings such as **foretell, speak, and divine** (as in divination).

But what does a witch do? We may have been taught to connect witchcraft with darker things such as evil, Satanism, and manipulation, but only the last word is correct. A witch **does** manipulate things but only within themselves. Then, we resonate the effects of that change outward into the world. Just like a practitioner of meditation, yoga, or physical exercise, who changes the inner workings of their mind and body through regular practice, so does a witch align themselves with the natural world around them. Such is the nature of Pagan religions, including Wicca.

There are many forms of modern Pagan practice; Wicca is one of them.

The birth of Wicca as a modern religion can be traced back to the writings of a retired British civil servant, Gerald Gardner—in fact, there is an entire branch of Wiccan practice devoted to him called Gardnerian Wicca. He published his definitive book on the subject, **Witchcraft Today** back in 1954. Gardner also founded a coven—essentially a prayer/workgroup for witches, numbering anywhere from four to 40 members or more—and several members of his coven went on to publish books on the subject of witchcraft and magical living.

In Gardnerian and other traditional practices, a coven is led by a priest and priestess, who oversee the ceremonial Sabbath rituals and often represent the god and goddess during these rituals. They are also in charge of educating newer members of the coven and helping members move upward in the steps of a witch's formal education and life—wiccaning (naming), hand fasting, croning, etc.

The Wiccan Rede and the Threefold Law

Here we have one of many examples of similarities between Wicca and Judeo-Christian faiths. The Wiccan Rede is essentially the Golden Rule, worded as such: "Do what ye will, that it harm none." There is, so far, no evidence of this rede (rede means guidance or wisdom) in Ancient European pagan practices, but it is believed to have been penned by one of Gardner's coven members, Doreen Valiente.

The Wiccan Rede is in itself at the core of Wiccan philosophy—when it comes to spell-casting and daily life, a Wiccan makes a concerted effort to cause no harm. At the very least, malevolent intent is never a part of a Wiccan's practice—at best, this outlook causes them to live their lives with a purpose to add positivity to the world, and not increase the already-present negativity. Examples of this include volunteering, living green and recycling, fostering, and taking time for self-care and reflection. There is a touch of Buddhism and Eastern philosophy in this mindset, and while admittedly, it may very well be impossible to go through one's day without accidentally stepping on a bug or using single-use plastic, the goal of the Wiccan Rede is to try one's best and never **intentionally** harm. It has been said that "white magic is pretty; but black magic works," but at the true heart of Wicca lies the belief that by following the natural

8

laws and mimicking them in one's magical practices, one can achieve peace and happiness in life.

The Threefold Law states that whatever you do comes back to you, times three. Think of a pond when you throw a stone into it, and the subsequent ripples that slowly emerge to touch the shoreline. This basic tenet holds you to be accountable for your actions; whatever you do has consequences, so live mindfully and responsibly.

But the natural world can be violent sometimes, right? True. The natural world involves catastrophic storms, predator animals hunting prey animals, baby loggerhead turtles marching stoically towards the inland rather than the sea. Wicca takes us to task for being mindful, thoughtful creatures—it asks us to revere and respect the natural world, and make the conscious decision not to add to its disasters or calamities. A Wiccan will stop his or her car to help a turtle across the road, and will often be a more empathic, supportive parent to their children. Wiccans are merely human, however, and so additional words have been written to ensure followers of Wicca do not abuse the power that they've learned to harness: **neither "By the power of three, to cause harm nor to cause harm to me."** All spell craft must be devoid of harmful intent, or else simply—it is not Wicca.

A Faith of Acceptance

One of the things that draw people to Wicca is the fact that anyone can join. Men and women of any background, gender identity or sexuality are welcome. In addition, both the god and the goddess are recognized within each of us—instead of faith and ritual being highly gender-restrictive, it's understood that the god and the goddess represent the polarity and flow of energy within each being on Earth. Men can be caring fathers and express their emotions; women can be mighty and fierce and still considered feminine. Practitioners of Wicca are taught to understand that they both manifest the god and the goddess as well as learn from them on a daily basis.

In addition to accepting all who would want to enter the ways of Wicca, the Wiccan faith does not dictate how that new follower should practice his or her faith; many Wiccans prefer to practice in the privacy of their homes, while others still prefer to find a coven or larger community group to celebrate the Sabbaths with (Sabbaths are holidays throughout the year as well as full moon gatherings). While some Wiccans consider them monotheists and look at the power of the universe as a single deity, and all of the gods' and goddesses' **aspects** of that greater power, others consider themselves polytheists. Some Wiccans find themselves called to the Egyptian gods, others pray to Celtic ones, and still others to Asian nature spirits. The choice is up to the practitioner and no other Wiccan judges the next for how they follow their faith.

Living in the "Now"

Unlike other faiths, Wicca doesn't use threats to coerce its followers to practice better behavior. Life is not considered a proving-ground for a VIP-only afterlife. Life is the lesson, the daily chance to live well and to live in harmony with one's surroundings. There is forgiveness in each day—just as the Sun will always rise, so does a Wiccan realize that there is always time for a change for the better, and their connection with the god/goddess and nature can help ease them through difficult times, and towards a better life.

This is not to say that Wiccans don't believe in an afterlife. The afterlife is often referred to as "The Summerland's," and it does keep with other faiths in believing that the afterlife is a place of gentle repose, more forgiving than one's mortal life, but Wicca holds that all retire there in equality and peace.

Common Misconceptions about Wicca

Approximately one and a half million pagans are living in the US according to a 2014 study, and approximately one hundred thousand living in the UK, not to mention pagans living and practicing their faiths in Scandinavia, South America, Canada, Italy, and other countries of the EU. Even though those numbers are impressive, modern paganism (also known as "neo-paganism") is a collection of faiths that are considered a minority in comparison to Abrahamic religions such as Christianity, Judaism, and Islam.

What happens most often when you have a majority and a minority? Misconceptions—and what we don't understand we often tend to fear, or even spread rumors about.

The Pentacle and Pentagram. A pentagram is a five-pointed star; it can be inverse or right-side up. A pentacle is a five-pointed star set within a circle. While some believe these are the signs of Satanist beliefs, nothing could be further from the truth.

A pentagram with the star's single point right-side up symbolizes humanity. If you look at one, you can see a figure standing tall, arms and legs outstretched. The pentagram and pentacle serve as a tool to remind us of the power and potential of humanity. As children of the god and goddess, we are imbued with sacred gifts that help us to connect to ourselves, nature, and the universe beyond should we choose to learn about and use these gifts.

A pentagram is often the starting point for ancient talismans, such as those one would find in the Key of Solomon. In ancient times, these talismans were used for purposes ranging from drawing upon the power of the Moon to calling angels to help with aid, to extending life and strengthening one's health.

A pentagram with the two bottom-most points right-side up is often mistaken for the sign of the Devil. The Devil is a construct of Christianity's teachings, and not part of any pagan practice. The so-called "upside down" pentagram invokes the wild spirit of nature by showing us a horned animal, as well as reminding us of the Horned God—a pagan deity representative of nature, hunting, and the beasts we share the Earth with. Some pagans and Wiccans use the reversed pentagram when they want to get closer to nature.

The ancient symbol of the pentagram is also found and used extensively in tarot, particularly in the iconic Rider-Waite tarot deck first published in 1909.

Wiccans (and Pagans) Are Overly Sexual. This too is a common misconception. The difference here is that Wiccans understand sex is not connected with "sin"—in fact, being human by nature is not a sinful thing. We are all capable of malice, to some extent, and we must learn to live responsibly as adults—especially if we are not taught to do so as children. In the pagan faith, sex is a vital part of being human, but only consensually. It is to be respected as a sacred act, even if in a casual moment. Sexuality gives us life, but more importantly, it gives us touch, intimacy, and human connection. That being said, sex is not a necessary part of any pagan faith, including Wicca—being celibate is respected just as much as being polyamorous—but when sex between two adults occurs, it is done with respect, and always consent.

Wiccans Cast Spells. This misconception is true! Often the image that is conjured (pun intended) is quite different than the actual practice. A Wiccan casts a spell with a very specific purpose in mind and does so after some research, preparation, and a peaceful heart. Most importantly, a Wiccan casts a spell knowing there will be consequences for that magic released into the world, and would never cast a spell that would bring harm into an already chaotic world.

Think of a spell not as "magic" in the Judeo-Christian sense, but as a tool of focus. Just as mantras, prayers, therapy, and manifestation help us achieve greater things in our lives, so doe's magic for pagans and Wiccans. Humans are tool-using creatures, and magic is just one of those tools.

Wiccans Are Satanists. This is probably the most common myth. Wiccans do not believe in the Devil or Satan as a deity; these are Christian ideas. There is, however, a religion called Satanism, and it's more concerned with how a person acts and treats other people than anything else, but it is definitely not a pagan faith, nor is it Wicca.

Wiccans Conjure Demons. This edge of the supernatural world can be a little scary, admittedly, but no self-respecting Wiccan is keen on dabbling in conjuring beings that frankly

13

nobody understands particularly well. While many Wiccans and pagans do believe in the supernatural world—ghosts, angels, and other things that might or might not go bump in the night—they do not actively try to recruit them to get the housework done or wilt their neighbor's roses. The Wiccan Rede, the Threefold Law, and just plain, old common sense recommends otherwise!

Wiccans Always Wear Black. This is perhaps a silly myth, but still relatively active thanks to television and movies depicting witches. Wiccans wear whatever they like; some do prefer black, as black is a color of protection and shielding. Some Wiccans become much attuned to what is around them—including the energy of others—and black can help dampen that, somewhat. Other Wiccans prefer wearing white or lighter colors during a ritual, and still, others wear colors to match the current season of the year. Some Wiccans prefer to wear nothing at all, going "sky clad" during rituals—but this is either in the privacy of their home or among consenting members of their group or coven.

Chapter 1: Spells

Here we look at 5 powerful spells that you can use to help you attract wealth and increase your money.

Debt removal spell

Things needed

- Incense sticks in a smell of your choice (preferably sandal)
- 1 Purple candle (you can buy from a magic store or look online)
- Essential Oil of your choice
- Rolled parchment or paper, 6cms wide
- 1 unbreakable candle holder

Method

1. Place the incenses in an incense holder or just a deep narrow bottle and burn it.
2. Apply a little of the essential oil on your palm and run the candle over it.
3. Make sure you cover it completely from top to bottom.
4. Place it in the candle holder and apply the remaining oil on your body.
5. Now open the paper and write down all your debts.
6. Writ neatly and be sure to list every one of them. Remember to not leave out a single one and if you have problems remembering them, then you can look them up and list out each

and every one.

7. Reverse the paper and draw a pentagram on the back. A pentagram is a star that is drawn inside a circle and make sure that two of the pointy sides of the star are on the top with one at the bottom and one on either side.

8. Now pick up the candle and draw a pentagram on it using the pin or the burin and make sure you carve it out and that it is clearly visible.

9. Now roll up the parchment and place it inside the candle holder.

10. Insert the candle and make sure it tightly fits the holder.

11. Now close your eyes and call upon your deity.

12. Imagine that you are feeling very happy and invoking the deity for a good cause.

13. Now light up the candle and pick it up.

14. Walk towards the east and ask the god of air to help you banish away all your debts.

15. Now place it back down and sit in front of it.

16. Repeat you and say please let all my debts be banished.

17. Now wait patiently as the candles burns and even if you leave the room, come back before it burns out.

18. Allow the candle to light up the parchment paper and allow it to burn completely.

19. Stare at the piece of paper as it burns away and feel happy that your debts have burned.

20. Finish by thanking your gods.

21. *Remember that doing this might not make your*

debts disappear but will most definitely allow you to clear them easily and also help you come into money soon.

Money gambling spell

Things needed

- A photo of yourself (preferably you smiling)
- Four yellow candles
- A green candle
- An essential oil of your choice
- Frankincense or lavender incense
- 3 leaves from a pineapple
- 3 amber stones
- 5 different coins
- An offering bowl

Method

1. Start by cleansing yourself and apply a little essential oil on your palm and rub it all over your body.
2. Wear either a green dress or a white one and get ready to cast the spell.
3. Now sit down and draw a circle in front of you.
4. Call upon the deities that you seek to enlist the help of.
5. Place the yellow candles at all the main points on the circle.

6. Now place the green one in front of you.
7. Now place the pineapple leaves, the stone and the coins in the offering bowl and place it in front of you.
8. Now light up all the candles in front of you including the green one.
9. Now pick up the green candle and drop a drop of wax on your photo.
10. While you say this, imagine that money is coming to you and you are extremely happy.
11. Now imagine that you are winning at gambling and that you have received a lot of money by gambling.
12. Now slowly blow out all the candles and let them stay there.
13. *Now thank your deities and it is best that you do this ritual a little before gambling.*

Full moon money spell

This spell is quite simple yet very effective. It is to be performed during the full moon as it will have a lot more effect then. It will be even better if you perform it at midnight. This can be a group activity as it will help you perform the ritual better and everyone will benefit from it.

Things needed

- Green Candle
- Sandalwood oil/Patchouli essential oil

18

Method

1. Start by cleansing yourself and have a cleansing shower.
2. Make use of herbs to clean and scrub you.
3. Ask everyone in the group to do the same.
4. Now sit down in a circle and use a pin to write down the names of all the people that are participating in the ritual.
5. Next, place a little of the oil on your palm and run the candle up and down over it. Make sure the candle is fully covered in the oil.
6. Now place the candle on the ground and light it.
7. Hold hands and stand around it in a circle.
8. Close your eyes and imagine that all your energies are unified and they are being used to help improve your luck and money is being generated for all.
9. Imagine that this money is making its way to all of you and it is making you very happy.
10. Say this in unison as it will help you channelize all your energies. Now help it burn away completely.
11. Once done, thank your deity and finish the ritual.

Money protection spell

Things needed

- One green or gold candle
- One yellow candle
- A money coin (preferably your lucky coin)
- A large bowl with a lid with holes
- Rose or lavender essential oil

Method

1. Start by cleansing yourself and scrubbing yourself with an herb of your choice.
2. Now carry all your materials outside with you.
3. Take your green or gold candle and place some of the essential oil on your palm and cover the candle in it completely.
4. Light it up and allow it to develop a steady flame.
5. Close your eyes and call upon your deities that you wish to invoke for your ritual.
6. Now place it inside the bowl and cover it with the lid that has the holes.
7. Now cover one of the holes with your coin.
8. You can ideally place it over the middle hole as it will help the smoke coming out from the other holes surround and cover the coin completely.
9. While this happens, you can repeatedly chant "Money gain, No money lost, Let me gain, Let it be, Bring me more, So Mote it be"
10. Once done, simply take the lid off and allow the candle to keep burning.

11. Take the yellow candle and place it next to the gold or green and light it.
12. Replace the lid on top and cover the center hole with the coin.
13. Allow the smoke from both candles to cover the coin completely.
14. Now chant the saying "Goddess of protection, Please help me, Protect the money you see, And let it be, Thank you"
15. Visualize that all your money is safe and that there is no loss. You are able to save the money that you have and it is not being wasted on anything. There is new money coming in and even that is safe and not going anywhere.
16. Now close our eyes and blow out the candle and don't open it until the smoke from the candle dissipates.
17. *Finish the ritual by thanking your deities.*

Money charm

Things needed

- Five pumpkin seeds
- Three small Cinnamon sticks
- One dollar bill
- 1 Green cloth
- 1 Green candle
- Cinnamon or basil oil
- 1 Green ribbon

Method

1. This is to be performed on a Friday so might have to plan it in advance.
2. On the Friday evening, assemble all your ingredients.
3. Cleanse yourself with the shower and the herb rub and get ready.
4. Call upon the deity that you want to avail help from.
5. Now place the candle in your palm and rub it with the cinnamon or basil oil.
6. Does this as you stare at the dollar bill and visualize your account coming into money and that all your debts are fully paid for.
7. Imagine that the money is making its way into your account and that it is staying there.
8. Now place the candle down and light it and allow it to develop a steady flame.
9. Now quickly take the green cloth and place the pumpkin seeds, the cinnamon sticks and the dollar bill and fold the cloth three times.
10. Tie it using the ribbon and make sure that none of the contents fall out of it.
11. Now repeat this three times after you are done tying and blow out the candle.
12. Thank your deities for helping you and carry the pouch with you.
13. *Place the pouch in your wallet or you locker and believe that it will help you come into money and that this money will stay with you for a long time.*

Five Powerful Spells for Attracting Power

The previous chapter we saw how you can increase your wealth and attract money into your life. In this chapter, we will look at 5 spells that you can use to attain power and turn around your fortune.

Success spell

This spell is meant to help you improve your career and better your success in the work field.

Things needed

- A photo of yourself with a frame (make sure you are smiling)
- 4 green candles and one white candle
- Amber incense sticks
- 10 fresh bay leaves
- 2 green fluorite stones
- Money (dollar bills)
- An offering bowl

Method

1. Start by having a cleansing shower and try and use herbs to cleanse your body.
2. Apply a little essential oil on your palm and rub it all over your body.
3. Wear a loose white gown or wrap your body in white sheets.

4. Now sit down to perform the ritual and use the green candles and place them in a circle in front of you.
5. Place the white one in the center.
6. Next, place the incense sticks in the holder and place the holder on your left.
7. Place all the rest of the ingredients in a bowl.
8. Place your photograph in front of the white candle such that its light falls on your candle.
9. Close your eyes and call upon your deities that you need to help you with the process.
10. Now pick up the candle and light the incense sticks with it.
11. Now before placing it back, drop a drop of wax from the white candle on your photograph and place it back.
12. Now hold the bowl containing the ingredients and offer it to your photograph.
13. Say it three times and don't open your eyes until you are done.
14. Now close your eyes and visualize you making progress at work and being able to climb the ranks fast. Imagine you being the boss and being in power. You are extremely happy and have turned into a very powerful person in your company. You are also the owner of the company and the boss.
15. Once you are done visualizing and feel satisfied, simply blow out the candles and allow the incense sticks to completely burn out and don't blow them out.
16. *Once done, thank your deities for their support.*

Self-esteem spell

Things needed

- A bath tub or a tub enough to immerse you fully (you can also use a swimming pool)
- Lavender essential oil
- Jasmine essential oil
- An oil burner
- Seven green oak leaves (or basil, depending on the season)
- One purple candle
- One yellow candle
- Some Purple thread
- An envelope

Method

1. This ritual will need you to completely immerse yourself in water so be prepared for it.
2. Although you don't have to be clothed for it, wearing all white is acceptable.
3. Start by preparing the bath and maintain an ideal temperature. Make sure it is not too hot.
4. If you have a pool then you can heat the water and then start.
5. Place the candles around the tub and light them and call upon the deities that you want to help you.
6. Now drop the lavender oil into the bath and

stir it around.

7. Drop in the leaves and make your way into the tub or pool.

8. Now immerse yourself completely in it and hold your breath for seven seconds.

9. Now come out and open your mouth to breathe for seven seconds.

10. Now continue doing this and every time you go in, imagine that your lungs are filling up with a sort of golden colored light and that all your worries and troubles have left you.

11. Imagine that all your inhibitions and doubts about yourself have left you and you are free.

12. Do this seven times and stop.

13. Now close your eyes and imagine that a ball of light full of opportunities and healing powers has gathered on top of your head.

14. Imagine the ball of light passing down through you and that it has instilled all its qualities in you.

15. You are now feeling extremely relaxed and have no doubts about your esteem and worth.

16. Now chant "I have my mark to make, I have words to say. Let others hear the words I speak. And take self-doubt away. And it harm none, so be it"

17. Now close your eyes and say this as many times as you like.

18. Stop; blow out the candles and leave.

19. Now pick up the oak or basil leaves and use the purple thread to string them.

20. Place them in the envelope and place it either in your pocket or under your pillow and try to carry it everywhere that you go.

21. If you are to ever have a bad day where there is a lot of stress, the next morning, the first thing that you must do is to place the jasmine oil in the burner and burn it.

22. Burn the same candles, hold the same leaves up to the flame and repeat the chant seven times.

23. This will help you attain your self-esteem again.

24. You can repeat this ritual if the leaves completely dry out.

25. *Make sure you thank your deities after each ritual.*

Fortune spinning spell

Things needed

- Any Pendulum (enchanted, or Magic Crystal is better buy from magic store)
- A candle
- A piece of Paper
- Black Pen (blessed or regular buy from magic store)
- Or just a regular pencil

Method

1. Before you start this ritual, start by writing down the various questions that you have in mind about your past, present or future and everything that you want to know about it. Make sure the questions will have a yes or no answer to offer.

2. Start by cleansing yourself and wear a white gown.

3. Now sit down in a place and light the candles.

4. Place the paper in front of you and draw an arrow that is pointing upwards and draw it on the right hand side of the paper. Name this as "yes".

5. Draw an arrow pointing downwards on the left hand side of the paper. Name this is "no".

6. In the center, draw an arrow that is pointing both sides and so you can label it "unsure".

7. Now hold the pendulum in front of you and on top of the paper.

8. Now ask the question and allow the pendulum to rotate and move over the piece of paper.

9. Depending on what the answer is, the pendulum will start to swing in the direction of it.

10. So if your answer is yes then it will swing towards yes and if it is no then it will swing towards no.

11. Once you have all your answers you can blow out the candles and fold the paper.

12. Make sure you only stop after you have all the answers and then stop.

The weekly power spell

This spell is meant to help you remain lucky for the whole week and also attain power, wealth and fortune. You can

Things needed

- Black 7 day candle (buy from magic store)
- Water
- Patchouli essential oil
- saucer (plain or blessed)
- a piece of paper

Method

1. Start by cleansing yourself and applying some essential oils on your body.
2. Now sit down and fill your saucer with the water.
3. Make sure it is not overflowing and place it down carefully so that no water falls out.
4. Call upon the deities that you wish to invoke in order to help you.
5. Now with the pen and paper, write down what you wish to attain in the following 7 days and you can write it down day wise if you like.
6. Now fold the piece of paper and slowly immerse it in the water inside the saucer.
7. Make sure you don't try and remove the piece of paper out again and once immersed allow it to remain there.

8. Now take the candle and apply some patchouli oil over it.
9. Next, place the black candle on top of the piece of paper and light it.
10. Try and balance it or you can also use a small stand. Just make sure it is transparent.
11. Now burn the candle and visualize your entire week.
12. See that everything you want is coming your way and that your whole week is blessed.
13. You are able to attain all your goals and each one of your wish is coming true.
14. Now wait for the candle to completely burn out and even if you leave the room make sure you are there when it is extinguishing.
15. The next day, place another candle on the same spot and allow it to burn completely as well.
16. *Don't forget to thank your deities at the end.*

Power necklace charm

Things needed

- A drawn pentagram
- Pentagram necklace (make yours or buy from magic store)
- 2 white candles
- 1 purple candle

Method

1. Start by cleansing yourself and apply an essential oil of your choice.
2. Wear all-white attire and start with the ritual.
3. Call upon the deities that you wish to invoke and ask them to help you.
4. Raw a pentagram on the ground and use a piece of chalk or candle to do so.
5. Now place the white candles on opposing sides and make sure that one is in the east and the other is in the west.
6. Place the purple one in the north direction and place the pentagram necklace in the center of the pentagram.
7. Close your eyes while saying it and as soon as you are done, blow out all the candles at once and imagine that the smoke they emit contains a lot of power and this power is energizing your pendant.
8. Imagine that the pendant is now extremely powerful and it contains all the necessary requisites to make the wearer all powerful.
9. Gently lift the pendant and wear it around your neck.
10. Thank your deities and get up.
11. Remember to carry this necklace anywhere that you go and remember to never give it to anyone else.

Chapter 2: Wiccan Deities

When working with magic, it is important to plan your spells according to many factors. Additionally, it can be helpful to understand the symbolism and magic inherent in the plants and animals we see either in our dreams or waking life. This is a practical guide to understanding the meaning behind the aspects of the natural world, when to plan your magical work, and which plants and flowers might be useful to you in the circle.

Magic and the Phases of the Moon

The great part of following the Moon for your magical work is that you get a chance each month to manifest what you truly need.

New moons are a perfect time for beginnings, though they require a certain degree of courage and faith for you to move forward. Think deeply about your desires and plan ahead—imagine your future success. Magic involving purification, initiation, beginning a project or new union, are all excellent workings to be undertaken beneath the new moon. The new moon is pristine, pure in spirit—if you are planning to detox, discard a negative habit or begin a new diet or fitness routine, the new moon is also suitable for affirmations concerning these things.

Waxing moons are when the new moon is growing towards the full moon, and are wonderful times to do magical work concerning abundance, growth, strength, physical and mental health, and striving towards a long-awaited goal. Magic regarding career and finances are best undertaken beneath waxing moons; however, there is a time when an emergency dictates action. Just understand that the Moon's energy, combined with your spell craft, will yield a result of a particular kind. Magic to aid in the search for a new job may find you opportunities during the waxing moon; the same magic may cause you sudden, unexpected job **loss** during the waning moon—but such upheaval might also reveal an opportunity you would have never seen were you to be at the office that day.

Full moons are the culmination; the moon is at its strongest now, and psychic abilities are at their most sharp. A spell you begin several days or a week before the full moon can now be realized fully. Full moons can be time for celebration, concentration, and manifesting your dreams.

Waning moons are times of recovery, rest, and cleansing. Spell work undertaken beneath a waning moon will be about getting rid of what is not necessary for your life or shaking off whatever's holding you back from realizing your goals. Banishing or protection spells can be useful at this time as well.

Dark moons are the best times for spells of reflection, regarding personal growth. Do you crave to rise like the phoenix and shake off the binds of old habits and ways? A spell for renewal and personal insight during the dark moon can help lead the way.

Days of the Week

Sunday is a perfect day to do magical work regarding health, finances, fortune, and abundance—anything that you can imagine growing bigger with the Sun's light can be done on this day. Sunday's colors are orange, yellow, white, and blue. On this day, mother goddesses and sun gods can be called upon to aid you in your work.

Monday is a tricky day for magic, but it is a good time for beginnings. It's the day of the Moon—and by the Moon's light, we don't always see things accurately with **our eyes**, but we can often intuit them with our heart. Monday's colors are blue, red, and black—the Nigerian god Papa Legba—an African version of Mercury—is honored this day. Give him an apple, some coffee or cola, and some candy, and ask for his guidance or to help with an endeavor.

Tuesday is a day of battle and strength. Today is best for spells of protection or strength. Tuesday's colors are red and gold, but it is best not to wear red on your person this day.

Wednesday is a day of communication and being bold. Wear red somewhere on you to attract good fortune and luck. Magic involving trade, the arts, making beneficial connections, and receiving good news can be performed on this day.

Thursday is a day blessed by lucky Jupiter. The wheel of fortune tarot card favors this day. It is an excellent day for magic involving self-love, rejuvenation, manifesting wishes, and luck in business.

Friday is a day of love, but can also be a day of justice. It is ruled by **Venus** but is also a day thought to be sacred to **Oshun** and **Oya.** Magic involving trust and fidelity, healing, love and friendship, and justice for the innocent can be handled on this day.

Saturday is ruled by Saturn, and can be a heavy day to work with—but it is the **best** day for spells of protection. Keep in mind that in some practices it is **also** a day of love goddesses, which goes to show that magic involving romance must be utilized with great precaution.

Plants and Herbs

Apple. An apple contains a five-pointed star within it. Two halves of an apple can be shared between lovers to ensure fidelity. Applewood makes excellent wands. Use apple blossoms in love and healing sachets, potions, and incense.

Acorn. The acorn symbolizes the love between the god and the goddess, as well as nourishment. Use acorns in spell work involving money, success, fertility, and good fortune. An acorn can also be used to increase the potency of a spell.

African violet. Use African violets in spells of protection, in charms to appease the faeries, and to raise the positive energy in your home.

Alder. In Norse mythos, the woman was created from the Alder. Use this wood in work involving courage, confidence, and charisma. Also, good for journeys—literal and metaphorical.

Alfalfa. Alfalfa increases the potency of the other herbs being used in magical work, especially when it comes to money. Burn alfalfa and sprinkle the ashes around the outside of your home for money luck.

Allspice. This spice can draw money to you and help with a successful business. It can also foster peace in the home and in one's mind. It can also be used in spells to benefit one's overall physical health.

Almond. Use almonds in works for abundance, healing, and mental sharpness.

Aloe. This plant is imbued with the energy of the Moon. It is perfect to use in spells having to do with beauty and wellbeing. When kept around the house it guards against misfortune.

Alyssum. This beautiful, tiny flower helps our grounding energy and lends a gentle comfort to our work. Perfect for magical work having to do with healing and peace

Amaranth. The eye-catching, crimson tongues of this plant always draw attention in the garden. It is a token of both the spirit world and the Mother goddess. Make wreaths of it to promote healing in the household, and use on your altar to honor the dead in their journey to the Summerland's.

Angelica. Use the root of this plant to banish negativity and usher in positivity. It has the power to connect us with the angelic world.

Anise. This fragrant seed can be sewn into dream pillows to ward away bad dreams. Used in sachets around one's room, anise will protect against evil and ill intent.

Arnica. The flowers of this herb can help sharpen psychic abilities.

Ash. A favorite wood for wands and brooms. The leaves can be carried for luck or placed in pillows in order to have dreams of the future.

Asparagus. The humble asparagus can be used in fertility spells to increase male stamina and virility.

Basil. A wonderful herb, basil can be used in money magic, as well as in home protection. When used in love magic, it can soothe inflamed tempers and help make peace between lovers.

Bay Laurel. Bay leaves have many purposes. You can write a wish on a bay leaf and toss it into a bonfire; it can also be used to exorcize a space of any negative energy, especially when combined with sandalwood. Adding a bay leaf to a magic sachet or other herbal spell will increase its potency.

Bayberry. This plant is perfect when blessing a home, and at Yule for magical wishes. It helps with good luck, successful business decisions, and wealth in general.

Betony. Grow this plant around the house for protection and to reverse hexes.

Birch. This wood is sacred to Beltane and Ostara and has been connected with the Norse world tree. In magical work, it can be used in cleansing, new beginnings, fertility spells, and the calming of upset emotions.

Bloodroot. This wild-harvested plant can reunite severed ties in families, as well as bring peace to the home in general.

Burdock. Use in healing rituals and baths, as well as for protection and to keep negativity at bay.

Cardamom. Use in love and lust magic, and for spells to help you appear more charming to an audience.

Chamomile. Connected to the Sun god. Use in money magic, as well as for purification. Making a floor wash with chamomile and scrubbing doors and windows, you can protect a house from unwanted entities.

Chestnut. Use in magical work for success, as this tree is sacred to Jupiter

Chickweed. Another wild-growing plant, chickweed is not only edible, but it increases kidney health and function. Use it in magic that seeks balance and community.

Chrysanthemum. Another flower connected to the Sun god and the element of Fire. Use to decorate the altar during Samhain. Make a potpourri of the flowers to burn as a house blessing.

Cinnamon. Use in charms for love, success, and money. Cinnamon "warms" the energy of whatever it is near so it can increase the speed in which a spell takes to manifest, as well as make a living area seem cozier. It is connected to the masculine and can help increase male libido.

Cloves. It is another fire spice. It can be used in spells for good luck and to attract prosperity. Clove oil can be added to a mojo bag to increase its potency.

Comfrey. Use in magic that protects against theft, and for safe travels.

Corn. Blessed by the Mother goddess and aligned with the element of Fire. A perfect offering during a ritual, corn can be used in abundance and luck spells.

Crocus. It can be used for magical work regarding hope, new beginnings, and peace.

Daisy. To be used in decorations and wreaths during any warm-weather Sabbath, as well as in divination spells.

Dandelion. Increases psychic ability and helps in connecting to the spirit world.

Deadnettle. This beautiful plant grows prolifically in early spring. It is called "dead" because, as a nettle, it does not sting. It is used in grounding magic and removing obstacles.

Echinacea. It is also known as the coneflower. Just like bay leaves, cinnamon and alfalfa, Echinacea increases a spell's potency. Cut flowers in the home draw prosperity. Use in magical work for inner strength.

Evening primrose. Use in spells regarding better self-confidence. It can also be used to bless an upcoming hunt, as well as in success in your endeavors.

Eyebright. Use in magical work for clarity and objectivity. It is an excellent altar decoration, especially for Samhain and at handfastings.

Fennel. Use in love and healing charms and to help with psychic abilities. It can also be used to protect against hexes and for courage.

Feverfew. Use for safe travels and to break hexes. Grow

outside your front door to keep illnesses from entering your home.

Forget Me Not. Use in loves spells.

Garlic. Use in protection spells. Stick three pins through a clove of garlic and sew (carefully) into a red cloth to hang at each exterior door and you will keep evil away from your home.

Geranium. Use to keep yourself protected from any unwanted love magic. Incorporate a piece of geranium root into a sachet or amulet to attract prosperity and joy.

Goldenrod. If goldenrod blooms near your door, money and good fortune are headed your way. The belief that goldenrod increases allergies is a myth; it does not spread its seeds through the air. Use in money magic. Make a wreath to keep inside the door to keep evil away.

Hazel. This wood can be used in healing magic. It is pure wood, and hazelnuts on a string can enlist the cooperation and aid of faeries of the field.

Heather. Heather kept in the house attracts helpful, benevolent spirits. In the garden, heather will attract helpful faeries. Toss into a Litha fire for good fortune and vitality.

Holly. This is a perfect wood for wands. Use in the home during winter to invite faerie folk to warm themselves at your hearth, but burn the holly at Imbolc to ensure they do not become permanent housemates. Use holly for money magic, good luck, and magical dreams.

Honeysuckle. Another good flower for faerie magic, honeysuckle also can be used in spells concerning love and devotion, as well as psychic visions.

Honey Locust. Also known as thorny locust, these trees produce spikes that protect the faeries from unwanted visitors. It can be used to keep imminent danger from home, but ask the faeries permission first, and leave an offering of honey and milk at the tree's base.

Indigo. It can be used in binding spells.

Ivy. Ivy offers protection to women if carried by them, and protects against disaster when grown beside a home. Use in spells of protection and healing.

Juniper. Carry seven juniper berries in a sachet in your pocket for a week for good luck; on the seventh day, toss them into fresh soil or a fire, and your luck will increase even more. Use in blessings, purification magic, and for protection against invading spirits.

Lavender. Use in love and money spells, and to lighten the spirits and raise the energy of a home.

Maple. Use in magical work for safe travels. It is also good for students to increase their potential, and for healing.

Marigold. It can be used for protection magic in the home. Also increases fertility in couples when carried in a sachet. Use for prophetic magic and in magic regarding legal issues or business.

Mint. Use in healing magic and to soothe hot tempers.

Mistletoe. It is sacred to Yule and Midsummer, and both the god and the goddess. Use in love and protection magic, as well as for spells concerning reconciliation. Hang in the house to keep negativity away and attract love.

Mugwort. Use in spells for prophetic dreams, divination, and dealing with difficult truths. Do not ingest mugwort and take care in handling it, as it has psychoactive properties.

Nettle. Also known as stinging nettle, use gloves when harvesting nettle. Doused in boiling water, nettle's stings are instantly softened and rendered harmless, and it can be eaten like spinach. Its vitamins and healthful properties are many. Use nettles magically to drive out unwanted spirits and negative energy. It can also be used to break curses.

Nutmeg. Use for good luck while traveling, for successful court cases, and luck in games of chance.

Oregano. Use in magical works for greater happiness and luck, also in protection spells. Fresh sprigs are wonderful decorations for the altar during joyful ceremonies.

Parsley. Use to connect with the dead and the spirit world. A masculine herb, parsley is beloved by love goddesses. Use for spells concerning vitality.

Pennyroyal. Use in protection and healing spells, and for aura cleansing.

Phlox. Decorations using phlox are welcomed at any spring Sabbath. Use in spells for greater courage and to increase productivity.

Plantain. This wild plant heals insect stings, cuts, and rashes, and can be used in healing magic as well.

Potato. Use in protection and grounding magic. Cutting a potato into quarters and burying each piece at a corner of your property is said to protect against misfortune.

Rice. Use in money and prosperity magic; mix with gold and silver glitter or paint. An old practice is to keep a container of rice at the door of a home; evil spirits will become consumed by counting the grains, and forget to enter.

Rose. Use in magical spells regarding love, beauty, and self-esteem.

Rosemary. A wonderfully protective plant, rosemary can be burned in lieu of sage to cleanse a space spiritually. It also ensures potency and successful magic when combined with other herbs.

Rue. Bunches of rue can be used to rid a person of negativity by rubbing it over them. Rue candles are wonderful when used in conjunction with a spell to gain your heart's desire.

Saffron. Use saffron in spells for wealth and recognition. It can also increase psychic abilities.

Sage. A sacred herb used by many cultures, sage cleanses a space and purifies it for magical work, as well as connects us to the spirit world and our ancestors.

Solomon's Seal. Use in spells for protection, transition, and changing bad habits into good ones. An amulet with Solomon's seal can ward off evil.

St. John's Wort. Use to banish depression and darkness from the spirit. St. John's Wort can also be used to rid a house of mischievous or malevolent spirits.

Tansy. Use in rejuvenation magic, and for spells to aid communication.

Thyme. Incorporate thyme into money-drawing sachets. Use in spells for courage and good health. Planted in your garden, thyme will attract the faeries.

Valerian. Use for prophetic, happier dreams and to connect with animal spirits.

Vervain. A sacred plant, vervain is used for protection, to open psychic awareness, and cleanse magical tools. It brings blessings and attracts good fortune.

Violet. It is for use in love spells, protection, healing, and wishes coming true.

Walnut. It is for prosperity and wealth. Keep a bowl of chestnuts in the home, and you will always have wealth coming into your home.

Water Lily. Use to communicate with water elementals and for moon magic.

Yarrow. Use in divination magic as a tea. A bunch of yarrows hung in a bedroom protects the person who sleeps there.

Yew. Use in protection magic and to decorate the Yule altar. Do not burn yew, as it releases poisonous smoke.

Animals

Cardinal. There is no chance you will miss the spiritual message of a cardinal catching your eye. A cardinal lets us know that it is okay to be bold and go for what you want. Its crest connects it to the spiritual realm, and as such, it remains connected to both the material and spiritual plane. Courage and decisiveness are not bad things; you can be ambitious, and also spiritual.

Take some time to learn about who you truly are, and how you can make peace with that. Play to your strengths and don't be ashamed of your weakness. A true leader knows when to listen, as well as to call out to his or her followers.

Chickadee. Chickadees bring news of the future and happiness on its way. They are daring, confident and opportunistic creatures, taking what they need at the moment as well as socializing in a mixed-species flock when it is not mating season. Chickadees remind us to branch out into the world and make connections when we can.

The chickadee also teaches us to be flexible and go with the changes life brings us. Adopt a mindset of plenty, and you will never want for anything—avoid a scarcity mindset, as each day holds great potential.

Duck. When the duck visits us (or catches our attention), it reminds us to look at our surroundings with fresh eyes, as there might be an opportunity or two that we are missing. The duck also seeks to teach us that brotherhood, sisterhoods, and family, are all important, and it's not always blood that connects us.

The duck also lets us know that it is okay to keep going at the pace we have been traveling—faster is not always better. We will get to our goals when it's the right time, for **us.**

Another message of the duck is to have the courage to explore our emotions. Perhaps we have been ignoring that part of ourselves. Now is the right time to examine them.

Eagle. This magnificent bird, when it visits us, implores us to reach higher than we ever thought we could. You have the potential and power for greatness, and to lead. Part of that potential is a sense of humility and modesty. A great leader has compassion and uses his or her power only when necessary.

In addition to leadership, the eagle shows us that it is possible for our abilities to take us to great heights. It is time to enjoy the freedom that comes from soaring among the clouds.

Hawk. The hawk brings us messages from the divine and the angelic plane. Work with divination and hone your skills regarding scurrying, tarot, or whichever method calls to you the most. Do not be afraid to try.

Now is the time to listen to your intuition and your gut. Important messages are waiting for you. Place importance on your vision and don't ignore your ideas or observations.

Owl. Hearing an owl traditionally means that others are having conversations about you. When you see an owl in your waking or dream life, it is calling you to understand that not everything will be revealed at this time. The owl is a creature of the Moon and the darkness and flies among the shrouds of mystery. Wisdom comes from experience, over time—not because we demand that it reveal to us its secrets. Have patience when an owl visits you, and open your mind to what the universe has to teach you.

Mockingbird. The mockingbird comes to us when we have perhaps lost our way, and forgotten who we are. It beckons us to recognize that we long to return to innocence—not innocence as in the opposite of sin, but innocence as in who we were when we were born. Each of us is a unique soul, a seed filled to the brim with potential. Take time to examine what you really want in life, and fill your head with dreams of manifesting that desire.

The mockingbird is a symbol of the artist in his or her ability to see the world and translates it into art for others to enjoy and recognize. Find your voice and show the world the truth that you see in it.

Robin. When a robin appears to us, we are reminded to get rid of whatever is cluttering our spirit. We must let go of the past in order to ensure a bright future.

Swan. To see a swan foretells of good luck, new love, and good fortune. A pair of mated swans signifies a happy union.

Turkey vulture. The turkey vulture, despite its reputation, is a benevolent creature. It symbolizes rebirth and the Crone—the decay that is inevitable in death feeds the Earth, enabling new life to appear. If you notice the turkey vulture in daily life or dreams, be reassured that you too are slowly being reborn. Now is a time of renewal for you. You have survived, and soon, you will thrive.

Cat. While the rest of the world holds that a black cat

crossing one's path is bad luck, Wiccans and pagans know better.

When you spot an unfamiliar cat crossing your path, use a general rule of magical colors to decipher their message, with a black cat being an omen of good luck and good fortune.

Orange: Abundance, self-esteem, welcoming.

White: Messages from the divine; angels.

Gray: Neutrality and mystery; the matter is not yet decided.

Brown: Being grounded; the promise of potential.

Coyote. The coyote is a trickster animal. Tricksters should not be feared—they are great teachers. They strive to teach us not to be hypocrites and artfully to call out injustice where we find it. They also teach us that words often make better weapons than swords, so we should use them carefully.

Crow. The crow brings us messages of magic and mystery. We need to keep a sharp eye out for intuitions hidden on the wind.

Bear. Bears remind us to take advantage of the natural medicine the world has to offer—medicine as in remedies, but also as in magic and creator-energy. The bear prepares itself while others play. Make sure you are prepared for leaner times by taking a moment to gather what you need and store it in a safe place.

Dog. The dog reminds us that loyalty is a gift and should not be taken for granted; it also reminds us to enjoy the Sun and life's simple pleasures from time to time.

Deer. The deer brings us a message to listen to our senses. Keep a keen eye on the proverbial forest and use your abilities to avoid danger.

Elk. The elk reminds us that we are strong. Life requires stamina and endurance, and we have what it takes to go the distance.

Fox. The fox is a keen observer and asks us to have a sharper look at our relationships when it appears. The fox is a quick thinker and strategist and aligns his body with the North when diving for mice beneath the snow. Trust your gut and study your surroundings with a sharp eye.

Groundhog. The groundhog is a family animal, invested in his community and dependent on its neighbors. Perhaps it reminds you that community can be helpful, and an important source of support. Conversely, the groundhog also brings the message that complication and drama in life are simply unnecessary—you have a comfortable burrow safe in the earth in which you can connect with the goddess, so do not be afraid to withdraw once in a while.

Lynx. The elusive lynx reminds us that even the most deeply-buried secrets will eventually be revealed.

Opossum. The possum reminds us that sometimes taking no action is the best action to take. Patience in life is key when you see an opossum.

Raccoon. These mischievous messengers come to remind us that there is something we need to let go of, or that the universe has been trying to reach us and it is time to open our ears to its call.

Snake. The snake is a sacred animal of the goddess and brings us a message of fertility and rebirth. Not all fertility refers to childbirth—an artist or writer may benefit from their fertile imagination in creating new work, and an entrepreneur might hit the metaphorical fertile ground with an exciting new business idea. A new course in life might occur to someone who has been stuck in a rut for a while. Have hope—spring is on the way.

Whale. The whale brings us a message of ancient knowledge, and that our ancestors walk with us and guide us.

Wolf. The wolf brings us news of union and new bonds and lets us know that we can trust our intuition and guides as we embark on this new path.

Chapter 3: A Beginners Toolkit – Magical tools and Items

Acquiring new magical implements is undoubtedly a fun and exciting part of Wicca, but it is important to realize the true nature of tools. Take a look at the Magician tarot card, for instance: he holds a tool above his head, his arm extended. When it comes to tools, the question you must ask yourself is: **Where is the source of the power is it the tool, or the Magician?**

Of course, the correct answer is the Magician. To write a sentence, we could smudge our fingertip in some soot and write words, but those words might be clumsy, and difficult to read. Instead, we craft a pencil or pen, fine-tipped and precise—or build a printing press. Just as our mundane tools help us achieve what we desire, so do our magical tools serve us during times of ritual. It is not a green candle that will draw wealth to you—it is your will, and you use a candle with that corresponding color to **focus** your will for better results.

The Athame

The Hermetic Order of the Golden Dawn was one of the most powerful influences on Wicca as a modern religion and remains today an active organization that trains and teaches pupils in the study of magic and witchcraft. The Order's analysis of the athame is that it is a tool of Air, while others read the athame as a tool of Fire. The athame is a knife that is traditionally not kept sharp—it is meant for cutting only symbolically—but because it is still a knife, and knives cut, the connection with Air remains, as the intellect often has the power to cut through confusion.

51

The connection to Fire holds that knives are forged with fire. This being said, a modern athame can be crafted from a wide variety of materials, such as wood, stone, stainless steel or iron, and even resin.

When choosing your athame for your altar space, you may opt for the traditional black-handled, metal dagger, or go for something more creative. There is no wrong choice. Try to keep in mind that an athame is meant to be short—merely a hand's length. Swords and longer blades are different tools for different purposes, and not recommended for the beginning witch.

If you happen to have a household knife that feels good in your hand, feel free to designate this as your athame. The **feeling** of a magical tool is the most important aspect of it. It should be an extension of yourself, particularly your magical self. If you do choose to use a household knife as your athame then it can become dual-purposed; traditionally, athames do not cut things in ritual, but a sharp enough knives can be used to harvest magical herbs from your garden just as well. If you would rather keep with tradition, you can acquire a similarly-sized sharp knife called a **boline**, which is used for practical purposes, while the athame is saved for rituals. The boline is typically white handled.

When choosing your athame, you may opt to order it online, but if you can visit a shop or craft person's workspace, it helps to be able to hold it in your hand before making a decision. First, decide what this tool will represent in your circle—will it stand for Air or Fire? Then look inward at how you personally express this element. What speaks for you best, debate or poetry? Passion or quiet contemplation? When you hold your would-be athame in your hand, does it feel like a continuation of your thoughts?

Keep local laws in mind. It is always research laws concerning carrying blades in public if you plan to take your athame to a public ritual.

How will I use my Athame? Common uses (think again of the Magician card) are when you are drawing your circle before a ritual and addressing each of the Elements—also called "calling the corners". As you address North, East, South, and West, you will point your athame to that direction, your magical self-reaching out to it in honor and recognition.

Always hold your blade horizontally rather than vertically. Try to keep it elevated on a level plane with your forehead (where your "third eye" is located). Your athame is used to cut energy symbolically—if, for instance, someone needs to leave a public circle during a ritual, a priest or helper will "cut" a doorway in the circle's protective energy so that person can step out, and will cut them back in when they return.

The athame also becomes a circuit of energy with your body as the generator. For this reason, if it is comfortable, hold your athame with both hands. Sometimes you will want to redirect energy back into the Earth, and in these moments, pointing the athame towards the ground is acceptable.

In ritual use, the athame represents divine masculine energy.

Bells

This is a lovely tradition in sacred spaces across the world.

The bell is the voice of the goddess, as well as your voice calling to her. A bell can be a beautiful means of focusing your mind on your task, and its sweet tones purify the space in which you are working. Small bells can be sewn into charms to activate them or hung from trees around your property to announce when the nature spirits are most lively or when the ancestors have come to give support.

Book of Shadows

Gerald Gardner introduced the concept of a personal witch's journal that kept track of their experiences, spell work, and anything else they observed or learned on their journey into Wicca. While he recommended that a witch's book of shadows is burned upon their death, in modern times such measures are not necessary for safety and privacy.

A grimoire is similar to a book of shadows, but it reads more like a formal spell book and less like a personal archive.

A book of shadows should be kept on or near your altar; it is undoubtedly the most important tool you will acquire. It does not have to be fancy, and you will likely need to purchase more than one, if not several, over time. Dates are handy and can show how much you have grown in your studies and practices.

With so much information available online for modern pagans, it may be useful to assemble one's book of shadows as a sort of scrapbook, with pages printed from websites; however, a useful tool in committing information to memory is the act of transcribing it. So, while you might save tips, advice, and spells from other Wiccans on your computer's hard drive, rewriting these pieces by hand into your book of shadows would be an admirable practice.

There are many beautifully-wrought blank books available, often leather bound, but even the most mundane composition book can work. The magic you put into your book of shadows will be all of your experiences.

The Broom or Besom

This magical tool has given rise to so much bad press about witches, and yet it is one of the most innocent and natural of magical tools found in most homes regardless of Wiccan practice or not. No one's really sure how legends of witches flying on brooms came to be, but as for hallucinations of flying—this has been present in every magical culture since the dawn of humanity, thanks to psychoactive ingredients found throughout the natural world in plants and animals. Nonetheless, a besom is a practical item used in Wicca to clear a space.

Let's talk about energy. You can think of energy, first of all, as something you can see, like light, blowing leaves, or dust. Energy comes and goes all the time—both negative and positive. Think of the last time you had a guest at your house that was too loud, too intrusive—perhaps they were curious about your things and felt the need to touch every one of them. Maybe your dog didn't like them. Whatever the case, remember how you felt **after they left?** Almost as if your home wasn't yours anymore, right? This is how negative energy lingers in a space. Fortunately, we have tools with which to get rid of that negativity and bring in fresher, more positive energy to take its place.

55

Energy also stagnates. Eastern philosophies warn against allowing clutter to accumulate, and this is because clutter becomes a visual symbol to us and invites stagnant energy to gather in our living spaces. Stagnant energy can lead to depression, lack of motivation, and fatigue.

Successful magic requires preparation. Just as you would rather start a busy day after a restful night's sleep and healthy breakfast, so should your magical spaces be cleaned of any stagnant or negative energy, and filled with healthy, bright energy and positivity.

Choosing a besom. Besoms of all varieties can be found in so many places; this might be the easiest tool that you can acquire. Home furnishing stores and country markets often sell handmade dusting brooms. Traditionally besoms are crafted from birch, willow, and ash, but anything that speaks to you is fine. Some Wiccans prefer to make their symbolic besom from a fallen branch that speaks to them during a walk outside.

To sweep a space free of negativity, use your besom a few inches from the ground and symbolically sweep in counterclockwise (also called **widdershins**) circles, also going counterclockwise around each room, while making your way towards an exterior door. Then sweep all of the energy you have gathered out of the house. Additionally, you can shake a little salt or pepper on the besom—or if you have pets, a small amount of salt water or Florida water.

Some folk knowledge and advice about the use of besoms holds that you should never use your besom at night, as this will sweep away your happiness, and you should not buy a besom in May. Never burn your besom! Doing so brings ill luck. Also, keep a dedicated porch broom for the outside areas of your home, and keep your besom for inside use only. Whenever you move house, leave the old besom behind and buy a new one for the new place.

The Cauldron

While the athame represents divine masculine, the cauldron symbolizes divine feminine energy. The cauldron in ancient times was a powerful symbol of nourishment, feeding families and villages with its never-ending richness. Its dark depths also depict the secrets of the womb and creation.

While the cauldron is an optional tool for Wiccan ritual, it is certainly handy for personal ritual work, and its applications are many. It can be used to hold burning incense safely, as well as hold a candle that must burn down completely to finish a spell. It can be used to "scry" or look into the future by filling it with water and gazing at its dark surface, and it can be used to gather rainwater or to charge water beneath a full moon for later magical purposes.

Your cauldron does not have to be traditionally sized, and many magical shops sell small, palm-sized cauldrons for personal use. Cauldrons made of iron can be expensive, and if your budget does not allow for a metal cauldron, a deep, round bowl can be used in its stead.

The Chalice (also called the goblet or cup)

The chalice is another symbol of the goddess and divine femininity. In community ritual, it often holds wine or grape juice to be passed around with cake or bread at the end with each person saying to the next never hunger, never thirst. It also is used in conjunction with the athame to recognize the union between god and goddess symbolically—the athame being ceremonially placed within the cup, blade first. The chalice is traditionally silver but can be any metal, or even wood or stone. Plastic is not recommended in magical use, as it is not grounded in the Earth (although it comes from petroleum mined from the Earth).

Treat your chalice with respect and keep it separate from your household cups. When you first bring your chalice home, you can cleanse it with salt water. It may also be left outside or on a windowsill during the full moon to "charge" it.

During ritual honoring a Sabbath or equinox, the chalice may be placed at the altar holding a libation suitable for the day, such as red wine or sangria for the dead at Samhain, mead at Yule, milk during Imbolc, cider during Beltane, and ale to celebrate Lammas. During a personal ritual, the chalice can hold water to recognize the Air element and the East or sit on the goddess' side as her representation.

The chalice is one of the most ancient symbols of unity, fertility, and bonding oaths.

Mirrors and Crystal Balls

The word **scry** describes the ability to know, or realize. Scrying is not just being able to tell the future—think of it more as driving your car on the road with your regular headlights; scrying is when you turn your high beams on, thus enabling you to see further ahead in greater illumination.

Crystal balls can be expensive, but for many Wiccans, there is no better way than to scry simply. The practice of gazing into a crystal ball takes time, but learning to trust your intuition, in the long run, will be invaluable.

When you first purchase your crystal ball, you must cleanse it before use—either by using a saltwater solution or by burying it in the earth for one day. When you rinse it clean, imagine any negative energy running off of it, down the drain or into the ground.

Next, you will want to charge your crystal ball with positive energy. Holding it, imagine a ball of white light gathering in your sternum—this is where your heart chakra resides. Allow the ball of energy to move from you to the crystal, completely encapsulating it. When you feel ready, allow the energy to disappear, soaked up by the crystal. Now you are ready to scry with it.

Scrying is a learned skill, like skateboarding or driving a manual car, and it takes time and patience. Do not feel frustrated if at first, you do not see anything, or if you can't make sense of what you have seen. It is a good idea to write down any impressions in your Book of Shadows—a journal kept specifically to record your magical work, dreams, meditations, and things that you have learned from others.

One word of advice: do not let your crystal ball sit in direct sunlight, but when the Moon is full, set it out to charge beneath the Moon's light.

Mirrors, on the other hand, can soak up the sunlight and increase their power—just be careful not to set anything on fire while you are doing so. A mirror can also be used as a scrying tool, as well as used in spell work. A word of caution: many recommend using mirrors to reflect negative energy towards someone. As a beginner practitioner of magic **and** as a Wiccan, it is best if you leave such spell work alone. One small exception, for home protection, involves placing small mirrors facing outward in your windows, to keep bad luck and ill will away from your house.

Charging your mirror with the sun, on a sunny day, bring your mirror outdoors and hold it so that it catches the sunlight fully. Do not look into it and make sure it is not directed towards any combustible material. Keep your pets and children away from you as you do this. Allow the mirror to charge for **exactly** nine seconds. Once you are done, return it to your altar. You can use the sun-charged mirror in spells needing a potent dose of the Sun's energy.

Scrying with your mirror can offer you glimpses into past lives. Don't focus your gaze as you stare at yourself in the mirror. Imagine scenes, movement—where are you? What is around you? Take notes of these visions and see if you can piece them together, over time, for clues to who you were before.

Mirrors are often believed to be capable of becoming portals to other realms. This is why mirrors are covered when a house mourns for a loved one who has passed on so that the dead will not become confused on their journey to the Summerland's.

The Sword

A sword should be treated with care and respect, as even a blunt-edged sword can be dangerous. Swords are usually used to call the corners/Elements in large, group settings. The High Priest typically wields them, but any practitioner can do the honors. The sword is seen as a larger manifestation of the athame.

The Wand

The wand is a tool that is also sacred to the god and represents masculine energy, but of course, can be used by any practitioner of Wicca. The wand represents fiery power, though like the athame, is also linked with Air. It can be used as a portable, miniature version of a besom, to manipulate energy in a sweeping, circular fashion—albeit in the air within a circle. It can be used to direct energy from the witch to an item used in a spell—such as a charm, potion, sigil, or totem.

Finding a wand is as easy as taking a walk in the forest. Fallen timber is best, but if you feel called to take a live branch, always ask permission of the tree first, and consider leaving an offering of honey, milk, or fresh fruit. Once you bring your wand home, you may carve it smooth or sand it, infuse it with natural oils, or even carve symbols or runes into it. Take some time to research different trees and their magical correspondences (there is also a discussion of this in Chapter 5). Another option is to cut a piece of young bamboo, which makes a handy tube in which to place written runes, spells and blessings, and gemstones.

If you don't live close to nature, a wooden dowel purchased from a craft or hardware store can make a suitable wand. You may wrap the handle with decorative ribbon, cloth, or leather, and hollow out the tip carefully with a knife to insert a gemstone with some Super Glue, and perhaps copper or silver coiled wire to hold it in place.

With the wand, you have an opportunity to really customize your magical tool, so try and take advantage of that. It doesn't have to be highly decorated to be creatively yours—it just has to feel right in your hand. Remember that we give power to our magical tools, not vice versa; while a good craftsperson does lend their unique magic and energy into a tool, at the end of the day, it is you who should be imbuing that tool with your wonderful, personal energy.

The wand can also be used to cast a circle in lieu of an athame if you prefer.

A forked wand is called a "stang". This can come in handy in public gatherings and can be stuck into the ground or leaned against a tree to hold a medicine pouch or bag of herbs or implements. A good practice is to find a unique stang wherever you call home; instead of leaving it behind as you would a besom, take each stang with you to remember the place you once lived.

Tokens of the Natural World

In addition to the traditional magical tools, anything you find in the outdoors that speaks to you may be taken—with permission, of course—to be used in your sacred space and on your altar. Many Wiccans begin to acquire an impressive collection of walking sticks and stones—sometimes, this is the very first indication that a witch is a witch.

Air plants, feathers, river rocks, bones, anything found on a good walk or hike that aligns with your energy and your spirit guides can be charged with magical energy and used in ritual.

Caring For Your Magical Tools

Just as your home needs occasional tidying up energy-wise, so do your magical tools. Use your judgment as to which method of cleansing you prefer, and according to what your tool is made of: with salt water or Florida water (purchased at online or local root work and hoodoo shops, this light cologne is sacred to Oshun), with smoke such as sage, Palo Santo, or rosemary, with the running water of a fresh stream or river, or with the earth itself. Look to the holidays and moon cycles as to how often you need to cleanse your gear. The Wiccan calendar follows the natural cycle of the seasons and the Earth, so it makes a good guide for self-care and the care of your tools.

Your First Altar

The most important part of this chapter is to drive home the point that it is **you** who are the source of the magic. An experienced witch knows that he or she can perform a spell in the middle of nowhere, with nothing in the way of tools but their hands, heartfelt words, and good intent. So, if at first, your budget allows for precious little in the way of new things, do not let it deter you from pursuing your Wiccan path.

Your altar can be anything at all, placed in a space where you can have privacy. A wooden footstool can make a wonderful portable altar, as can a short bookshelf. A simple side table that can be moved into position in the middle of your room works well too.

If you are unsure of whom to worship at your new altar, do

not worry. A simple representation of the god and the goddess is a good start. Remember that these are twin aspects of the universe—yin and yang, dark and light. If you imagine a beautiful, feminine woman in flowing gowns and cascading hair as the goddess, then find a statuette or image of such a woman and place this on one side of your altar. If you prefer to focus on the symbolism of the feminine, find something circular, or the infinity symbol, to place there. It is perhaps a small vase of fresh cut flowers, or a dish of rich soil.

For the god's side of the altar, make similar choices. If you feel drawn to a human-like, heroic personification, then fetch that image to place there. If a beautiful, polished stone or shark's tooth, or a piece of wood from a mighty oak speaks to you and then use this instead.

Another option is to use two candles to signify the god and goddess. Good colors to start with for the god are green, brown, or gold. Goddess colors can be red, pink, lavender, blue, or silver. For some, using candles feels more in the moment, almost as if during the time the candles are burning, the living presence of the god and goddess are there with you while you perform your ritual.

The goddess should be placed on the side you feel is best, as with the god. Think of the attributes of both deities and link them with what the right and left represent at this moment, and for your magical work. The left represents intuition, receiving blessings, the powers of the Moon, and peace. The right represents action, logic, communication, and understanding. If your altar space is square or rectangular, the deities are each placed in the far right and left corners.

In the middle of the god and the goddess, place a focal point. This can be a white candle, a mirror, your crystal ball, or anything that you would like to see as you relax your body and gather your energy before doing your work.

If you choose to have representation of each of the Elements at your altar, move the god, goddess, and your focal point inward a little, and place your item for Earth at the top, your item for Air on the right-hand side, your item for Fire at the bottom (you may want to move it to the side just below Air if it has incense or a burning flame so that you don't have to reach over it or breathe the smoke), and your item for Water on the left. If you can determine where North is in your room, turn your altar so that your North aligns with the magnetic North. Your magical tools can come into play here: athame and wand for the East or the South, chalice for the West, and cauldron, crystal ball or mirror for the North.

If you are doing any spell work, have all of the ingredients close at hand, as well as something to write with, matches if need be, and you're Book of Shadows. A glass of water is a good idea too to keep you hydrated.

A note about matches: these are preferred when lighting candles over lighters, as sacred light should not be struck by metal. That being said, if all you have access to be a lighter, does not worry too much about it.

Altar cloths. Many Wiccans enjoy having a special cloth to drape over the altar first before setting the items upon it, especially if the furniture you are using has a dual purpose.

Chapter 4: Wiccan Rituals- Wiccaning, Hand fasting and stages of life and death

Wiccaning

A wiccaning is a ritual that welcomes a new baby into a Wiccan community. While it may have some similarities to baptism, a wiccaning is not a guarantee that the child will follow a Wiccan path. Pagan parents usually allow a child to grow closer to maturity before deciding what, if any, spiritual path they will take—though parents will often choose to bring children along to community worship and allow them to help out at home on Sabbaths and lunar observances. The pagan thought on life paths and spirituality is that it must always be a personal choice, not something your elders can or should make for you.

During a wiccaning, a child is introduced to the community and the gods, as well as the spirits of nature and the Elements. The goal here is to gather together in the promise to protect and raise this child in love and trust—it takes a community to watch over an innocent life and make sure it flourishes, realizing its inherent gifts. Just like a farmer watches a seed grow into a hardy plant, so does the community vow to guard the child and help it grow into his or her potential.

Usually, a wiccaning is performed on an esbat or a Sabbath celebration, but it can be performed whenever the parents choose. Each wiccaning is unique and often written by the parents or a coven member, but generally, the baby is introduced to the four Guardians (the four Elements), the god and the goddess, the ancestors, and the community, asking all to promise to love and guard this young life as it grows and learns.

After the ceremony, members of the coven and community may approach the child with blessings and/or gifts to bestow upon them, and the priest and priestess formally introduce the newly Wiccan child for all to see.

Coming of Age

Children all reach sexual maturity at different ages, but generally, a coming of age ceremony is performed when a boy is twelve or thirteen, and within a lunar cycle after a girl has her first menstrual cycle. The point of this ceremony is not to sexualize a child—because even in adolescence, children are still too innocent to fully grasp what it is to form an intimate bond with another—but to honor and recognize the transition that child is beginning to take, and to renew the promise of protection and guidance that was first made at that child's wiccaning. Adolescence can be a particularly crucial time in a child's development, and having a community to protect that child and impart onto them the wisdom of elders is a blessing.

Gifts of jewelry such as necklaces with spiritual symbols are common. Decorations of the altar might be tokens of fertility, such as pine cones or decorated eggs.

At this point in a child's life, if they believe they are ready to embark on a spiritual path, they might choose a craft name (witch name) for the community to address them by. The community also—while still recognizing that they are a child—will begin to address and regard them as an adult from this point onward, to prepare them for the rigors and responsibilities of adult life.

If the child feels they are ready to embark on their spiritual path, and believes that their path involves Wicca, the community may also choose to ask them a series of questions—the answers to which are oaths sworn lovingly to the god and/or goddess.

Initiation

An Initiation happens when someone—of any legal age—chooses to enter the path of Wicca and devote themselves spiritually to the god and goddess. There are several steps to an Initiation, and the first step is the Dedication. While practices vary from tradition to tradition and from coven to coven, generally speaking, once a person goes through a Dedication ceremony, he or she must wait a year and a day before they are formally initiated. Training may take longer than this, and depends, usually, on what the priest or priestess thinks of the Desiccant's progress and commitment. There is no shame in a magical education taking longer than what is considered standard. Just as in the natural world, things take as long as they need to take, depending on their nature.

Minors are usually not allowed to move forward into Initiation, though they may be permitted to have a Dedication. Because alcohol or tobacco might be offered to the god or goddess as a libation, such things are better off not being observed by children, but each coven makes their own decision regarding this.

Initiation and Degrees of Learning. Many Wiccan communities practice Degrees of Initiation. A First Degree Wiccan takes responsibility for them. A Second Degree Wiccan takes responsibility for their coven, and a Third Degree Wiccan takes responsibility for the entire Wiccan community. A priest of a coven must be a First Degree Initiate, but a high priest or high priestess must have achieved their Third Degree.

Hand fasting

To the Ancient Celts, hand fasting was originally a "trial period" of a year and a day, where a couple in love would live together as one to see if they could go the distance for a lifelong commitment. Now, in modern pagan practice, hand fasting is the pagan version of a marriage ceremony.

Vows. Most couples will write their vows and recite them in view of the community or coven. Some couples will also choose to rededicate themselves to the god and goddess.

Cords. After their vows, couples will clasp hands, and a cord will be wrapped loosely around their hands, signifying the joining together in union.

Jumping the broom. This tradition is originally an African practice that many pagan couples also incorporate into their hand fasting ceremonies.

Couples of all sexualities are welcomed by the Wiccan community to join in marriage. A hand fasting ceremony is separate from the legalities of a formal union, although many Wiccan priests and priestesses take the steps necessary to marry couples within their coven legally.

Hand parting

During hand fasting, couples pledge to remain together so long as their love lasts in truth. If the love wanes, it is acceptable for a couple to have a priest or priestess performs a hand-parting ceremony. During this ceremony, the marriage cord is cut, signifying that both parties are free to seek their newly-single paths.

Croning and Saging

These ceremonies are reserved for elder members of a coven, once they have achieved a point in their magical education where they can be a source of wisdom and learning for other members of the community. Some covens will also crone, sage, or elder a younger member who is fighting a serious illness, such as cancer, to gently and lovingly prepare them for the possibility of journeying to the Summerland's earlier than expected.

Croning is the term used for women, sagging for men, and eldering is a gender-neutral term, all for the same type of ceremony.

One thing that is looked at is how much the person has contributed to the community, and if they are in their second Saturn return (usually between the ages of 58 and 60). The ceremony is most often performed at Samhain when the Crone goddess holds court.

Eldering can be a helpful way to remind older coven members that they are still vital, useful, and well-loved in the community.

Passing Over

The most common time to perform a Passing Over ceremony is during Samhain when the Veil is thinnest, but any time during the year can be suitable. Often psych pomp—a spirit guide or god or goddess of death, may be called upon to guide the deceased to the Summerland's gently. Members of the community gather to offer their memories of the deceased and wish them safe passage to the afterlife. The altar is decorated with images of the deceased and their family, as well as flowerings and offerings of nourishment for the journey beyond the Veil.

Chapter 5: Sabbats

Winter Solstice (Yule): December 20-23

Considered in most Wiccan traditions to be the beginning of the year, the Winter Solstice is a celebration of the rebirth of the God. It is the shortest day of the year, offering a welcome reminder that even though the cold season is still just getting underway; it doesn't last forever, as the days will begin to lengthen again after this point. Some consider the first Full Moon after the Solstice to be the most powerful of the year. This is a festive holiday celebrating light, as well as preparation for a time of quiet, inner focus as the Earth rests from her labor.

Among many Wiccans the holiday is more commonly called "Yule," a name derived from midwinter festivals celebrated by Germanic tribes. "Yule" is still referenced in modern Christmas carols, and many of the traditions surrounding the Christian holiday, such as wreaths, Christmas trees, and caroling have their roots in these older traditions. It was common for the Christian churches to "adopt" pagan holidays, repurposing them for celebrating saints or important events, as a way of drawing people away from the Old Religion.

Imbolc: February 2

Imbolc marks the first stirrings of spring, as the long months of winter are nearly past. The Goddess is beginning her recovery after the birth of the God, and the lengthening days signal the strengthening of the God's power. Seeds begin to germinate, daffodils appear, and hibernating animals start to emerge from their slumber.

The name "Imbolc" is derived from an Old Irish word used to describe the pregnancy of ewes and has been sometimes translated as meaning "ewe's milk," in reference to the birthing of the first lambs of the season. It is also called "Candlemas," and sometimes "Brigid's Day" in Irish traditions. Associated with beginnings of growth, it's considered a festival of the Maiden.

Spring Equinox (Ostara): March 20-23

At the Spring Equinox, light and dark are finally equal again, and growth accelerates as both the light from the still-young God of the Sun and the fertility of the Earth grow more powerful. Gardening begins in earnest and trees send out blossoms to participate with the pollinating bees.

The name "Ostara" comes from the Saxon Easter, the Goddess of Spring and renewal. This is where the name Easter comes from, as this is another holiday that was "merged" with the Christian tradition.

Beltane: May 1

As spring begins to move into summer, the Goddess begins making her transition into the Mother aspect, and the God matures into his full potency. Beltane is a fire festival, and a celebration of love, sex, and reproduction. It's at this time that the Goddess couples with the God to ensure his rebirth after his death at the end of the life cycle. Fertility is at its height and the Earth prepares to flourish with new life.

The name "Beltane" comes from an ancient festival celebrated throughout the Celtic Isles that marked the beginning of summer, and is derived from an old Celtic word meaning "bright fire." The ancient Irish would light giant fires to purify and protect their cattle, and jumping over fires was considered a way to increase fertility and luck in the coming season.

Summer Solstice / Midsummer: June 20-23

Long considered one of the most magical times of the year, the Summer Solstice sees the God and the Goddess at the peak of their powers. The Sun is at its highest point and the days are at their longest. This is a celebration of the abundance of sunlight and warmth, and the physical manifestation of abundance as the year heads toward the first of the harvests. It's a time of ease and of brief rest after the work of planting and before the work of harvesting begins.

Some traditions call this Sabbat "Litha," a name traced back to an old Anglo-Saxon word for this time of year.

Lammas: August 1

Lammas marks the beginning of the harvest season. The first crops are brought in from the fields, the trees and plants begin dropping their fruits and seeds, and the days are growing shorter as the God's power begins to wane. This is a time for giving thanks for the abundance of the growing season as it begins to wind down.

The word Lammas stems from an old Anglo-Saxon word pairing meaning "loaf mass," and it was customary to bless fresh loaves of bread as a way of celebrating the harvest. Lammas is alternately known as "Lughnasa," after the traditional festivals in Ireland and Scotland held at this time to honor the Celtic god Lugh, who was associated with the Sun.

Autumn Equinox (Mabon): September 20-23

The harvest season is still in focus at the Autumn Equinox. The animals born during the year have matured, and the trees are beginning to lose their leaves. Preparations are made for the coming winter. The God is making his exit from the physical plane and heading toward his mythical death at Samhain, and his ultimate rebirth at Yule.

Samhain: October 31

Considered by many Wiccans to be the most important of the Sabbats, Samhain is the time when the part death plays in the cycle of life is acknowledged and honored. The word "Samhain" comes from old Irish and is thought by many to mean "Summer's end," though others trace it to a root word meaning "assembly," which may refer to the communal gathering of a pagan festival, especially during the harvest season. As the Sun aspect, the God retreats into the shadows as night begins to dominate the day. As the God of the Hunt, he is a reminder of the sacrifice of life that keeps us alive through the long winter months. The harvest is complete and the sacred nature of food is respected. Among some traditions this is viewed as the "Third Harvest."

Wiccan and other pagan traditions view Samhain as a point in the Wheel when the "veil" between the spiritual and material worlds is at its thinnest, and the days around Samhain are considered especially effective for divination activities of all kinds. Ancestors are honored and communicated with at this time. Many of the Halloween traditions still celebrated in contemporary cultures today can be traced back through the centuries to this festival. Pagans of the old times left food offerings for their ancestors, which became the modern custom of trick-or-treating. Jack-o-lanterns evolved from the practice of leaving candle-lit hollowed-out root vegetables to guide spirits visiting on Earth.

Some Wiccans in the Celtic traditions consider Samhain, as opposed to Yule, to be the beginning of the year, as the death and rebirth aspects of creation are seen to be inherently joined together—death opens the space for new life to take root. Honoring the ancient Celtic view of the year having a "light half" and a "dark half," their Wheel of the Year begins anew on this day, the first day of the dark half of the year.

Chapter 6: Wiccan Crystal Magic

Were you ever called a pyro in school, or made fun of for your love of fire? The truth is that you're not the only fire lover in this world. Fire is a big part of the Wiccan culture because it is one of the elements. We are so connected with fire because it is a part of nature. Just as we are connected with the earth, we may be even more connected with fire, because it is such an essential part of our lives and our spells.

Fire dances across the wilderness as if nothing blocks its path. It is dangerous, and it is beautiful at the same time, and if that doesn't leave you with terrified awe, I don't know what will. Because fire is one of the most mesmerizing wonders of nature, our ability to connect with it is astounding.

Why do we connect with fire so well? Or, perhaps because it is such an essential part of a lot of spells. We spend much time with it during spells that we've created a bond with it. There are multiple theories why we connect with fire, and no single one is correct. The bottom line is that it is an essential part of many Wiccan rituals, and that is why candles are used.

Candles in Wiccan Rituals

Candles are often used in many spells, but they are used even more so in ritual spells. A true ritual spell will have you open your circle with a candle that represents each element, and probably a white one as well for purification.

Candles are part of a Wiccan's necessary items to complete a majority of spells. They are always there and are never a waste. Even when they are not needed, some Wiccans prefer to open their circles with candles every time, rather than just open their circles by calling the elements, and that is perfectly okay. If you have the time, then there is no harm in setting up the candles every time.

If you have come this far in the Wicca series, and you do not see the importance of candles yet, then this book will change your mind. Being the fourth book in this series, you have already read about some spells that involve candles, but there are more rituals that are based on candles alone. Most people think of herbs when they think of Wicca spells and magic, but the truth is that candles are just as powerful if they are used correctly.

Wiccans often use candles to bring them prosperity or protection, or any number of other reasons that they need to perform a spell. Sometimes they use candles to light smudge sticks because candles have the steadiest flames.

Candles offer natural light right at your fingertips and can be used to find the things you need. You could even do a protection spell with the same candle you are using for light. Candles also heat things up, such as herbs when you need to have the herbs warmed so that they are primed and ready to be used. There are few limitations with candles.

Fire Magic

Fire magic is the magic we make using fire itself, rather than the color of a candle. This magic calls upon the element fire. An example of a fire spell is a warming spell when we are out in the cold. Fire magic is remarkable because you can feel the warmth of fire when you are nowhere near an open flame.

To use fire magic, you must be open to handling an element

without a circle. This can get very out of control and takes a lot of practice. However, if you are prepared to do it, you will find that there are some amazing things that you can do.

There are a lot of Wiccans that doubt you can really harness the power of the elements, and it is true to an extent from what I have seen. Example, you cannot start a fire without a spark, but once you get a little ember, you can call fire to you to emblazon that ember and keep it burning for a good while.

You can also call fire to you to help you get that pesky pilot light on your heater lit. Fire has also been called upon by witches, to protect you from harm. There are many spells for harnessing the raw power of fire that it is a little scary. If everyone were to try them at once, it could get a little out of control with how unpredictable fire can be.

The Role of Color

Color plays an important role with candle magic. If you get the wrong colored candle and try to do a spell, then you may end up with a completely different result. You could be trying to get more money, but if you choose a blue candle, then you may wake up with longer hair—you never know. Colors are important; there are only five colors of candles in Wiccan tradition. Black and Grey are for darker magic, and none of them will be covered in this book. You will also use subsets of colors, such as pink and orange. While Green and Purple are considered secondary or subset colors as well, each of those is a primary in Wicca because of their representation of an element.

Blue

Blue candles can increase wisdom. You use these when you want to know more about the world, and you want to open your mind to receiving information you would otherwise be closed off to. Blue candles can also bring happiness, and bring you prosperity when combined with a green candle. There are many other uses for this candle as well, such as helping you deal with stressful situations.

Green

Green candles are the money candles. It brings wealth and prosperity to you. If you are looking to make more money, there are a million spells out there, and I bet that ninety percent of them involve you using a green candle in some way or another. It also helps with healing. Just as it can help heal your broken finances, it can also help with healing your ailments. It can bring more love into your life, and banish immorality. Green is the symbol of hope, of a new beginning.

Yellow

Yellow candles are known as "pick me up" candles. What do you think of when you think of the color yellow? You think sunshine and daffodils and daisies and so many other bright and happy things, right? Yellow is great for warding off depression or bringing a depressed person out of an almost catatonic depressed state. Yellow candles can also add happiness and energy into a room. Yellow is great for sharpening the mind and perpetuating kindness and bringing in new friendships.

Red

This is the color of passion, strength and courage. This is the color you see when you are so angry that you could scream, and also the color you feel when you are so into someone that you feel your heart is going to explode. Red brings energy into a room. It brings motivation as well. Red candles are used in a lot of motivation spells because of the energy courage and strength that it brings.

Pink

This candle is for love spells—almost exclusively. Pink is for attracting love. Not only from others but yourself. It is for personal success as well. It can bring you the success you need in many different endeavors, whether they be business or love related.

Orange

The combination of yellow and red, it is a mixture of passion and happiness. It makes sense that this color would be perfect for healing broken relationships and mending friendships. It is also great when paired with a yellow candle to bring happiness into the room.

Purple

This is the color of clairvoyance. The color of divination and the color of magic itself. This color represents Spirit, the guiding light and the place where our magic comes from. This color can relieve the emotional pain that has built up over the years and can be a great calming color. Use it for meditation. It will bring you inner peace so you can concentrate. Not to mention it is a beautiful color all around due to the many different hues that it comes in, no two of them are even remotely similar.

White

White candles are for protection, purification, and healing. You should have a white candle lit any time you are doing a sort of bloodletting in a ritual. You are literally giving your DNA to whatever takes up your blood as an offering, and without a white candle, or purification, your blood could be offered to an evil spirit. Lighting a white candle is how you protect yourself. It creates a shield to keep the unwanted spirits away.

Color plays a major role in magic. Each color has an attribute, and each attribute is unique. Pick the right color to get the right result. Pick a color to focus your energy on because it is not just about color, it is about the energy that is associated with it, and how strongly your energy is connected to the candle's energy.

Stay connected to the basis of what you want the spell to do, and if you are trying to send your energy out to every candle, then you will have some problems because your energy will not be as strong as it would be if you were just focusing on one candle. The only exception is in a ritual where you must have the five elements and the white candle burning, or if you have to combine two candles for a certain spell to make it more powerful. If your spell only requires one candle color, then follow the spell. Always make sure that you have the right color.

Chapter 7: Symbols and Signs

Incense Accessories

Incense can be a big part of your spells. Sometimes you need it for air representation, and sometimes you need it as part of the spell. If you use incense, there are some things you may need for it. These are completely optional, and there are several options to choose from. However, you do not have to choose any of these items if you do not want to other than something to hold up the incense, so it does not burn anything. The incense itself is all you need for the spell, and it must be able to stand upright so that it doesn't burn things and so the smoke can go into the air to work its magic.

If you do want to deck out your incense a little more, here are a few things that will help you out.

Incense Oil

This is like an essential oil, but it is made specifically to be drawn up through the stick of the incense to make the smell and the smoke a lot stronger. You can use it on smokeless incense as well, but most spells call for smoking incense, as the smoke (not the scent) is what performs the magic most of the time. This oil works with smoking incense too, though. Use it if you need a little extra kick to your spell, to make it really stick to the object you need it to.

Incense Holder

There are several types of holders, and they are all useful. There are decorative holders, and there are holders that are not pretty, but that get the job done. There are holders that allow you to add oil or rocks. These holders keep your incense upright and can make it more pleasing to the eye as well as more enticing to the deities. Ultimately, you simply need something that will hold your incense up, but if you can find a holder that does the trick and that looks nice, especially if it matches your chalice and athame, you should definitely go with it.

Ash Catcher

If you have ever burnt incense, you know how frustrating it is to clean up the ash it leaves behind. The ash from an incense stick is very fine and disintegrates when it is touched. This leaves you feeling more like you are spreading it around than cleaning it up. However, there are ash catchers that will help with that. You can even get an incense holder that has an ash catcher built in; that is super helpful because you will have fewer problems when it comes time to clean up after a spell.

These are just a few of the items you can get as accessories to incense, but these are the most essential. There are several other accessories that hold no other function than to be decorative. These items are not useful in your spell.

Cauldron

This is often portrayed in movies about witches as something used to make potions or boil children. While a cauldron can be used to make potions, it is most often used to hold water for scrying or to burn all your herbs for a spell. Most cauldrons are not giant pots because they don't need to be big. You are not going to be boiling goats or children, so you do not need a giant cauldron. The only time you would need a cauldron big enough to fit a human is if you were turning it into a Halloween-themed Jacuzzi tub. The biggest cauldron you would need is no bigger than a quart, and even that is often more than enough room for what you require.

If you come across a spell that requires a giant cauldron, run in the other direction because the chances are that it is a dark magic spell and you do not want to dabble in dark magic at all. It can cost you your soul, and that is not something you want to gamble with.

Pentacle

This is an important part of the Wiccan religion. The pentacle is often confused with the pentagram when, in reality, they are two different things. The pentacle represents all that is pure and right in the world. It is surrounded by a circle and is upright. The five points represent the five elements, not the five layers of hell like the pentagram represents. The pentacle is often carved into magical tools to give them the proper energy so that the tools do not need to seek energy from undesirable entities. You should also have it carved into your altar. It is a good idea to use one to mark out your circle as well. The more you have, the more protected you are from demonic spirits trying to take over your magical spell and twist you into doing their bidding.

You can even wear the pentacle. You can get a pendant and have it on a necklace or a bracelet. In fact, both are great; a bracelet with several pentacle charms also helps. You can have it sewn into your robes or carved on your wand. There are so many options for wearing the pentacle that it is not funny. You can even have it printed on shoes. Of course, there is such a thing as overkill. If you have the pentacle printed on your shoes and sewn into your robe, you do not need jewelry covered in pentacles. You can save the jewelry for gemstones that will help the ritual spell of the night you are celebrating.

Gemstone Jewelry

There are several different gemstones you can wear during these rituals; which ones you choose depend on what you are trying to accomplish when you are performing the spell. The gemstones give the magic a boost because they can reflect energy as you are performing a spell. If you wear the right stones for the right ritual, you can release a powerful magic without using all the energy in your body. However, it is still a good idea to eat well and be well rested before any ritual because of the amount of energy it takes. You will probably be tired afterward, but that is okay because rituals can take a lot out of even a strong witch.

Gemstones will help reduce the amount of energy needed for a ritual so that you may need only a nap rather than to sleep for a full day and a half or more. Some people feel like they are going to go into a coma if they try to perform a ritual that is too complicated for their bodies. Avoid the comatose state; search for stones that are good for certain rituals and wear them shamelessly.

Jewelry with Sigils

Many Wiccans wear jewelry with sigils and wear them proudly. These are little symbols that represent the ritual you are going to perform. However, if you are already laden with jewelry, the sigils may be better left to robe decoration. You can hang them from the hem of your robe. Too much jewelry will counteract the productivity that the other types of jewelry bring to the spell.

Ritual Robes

A robe makes the ritual seem that much more official. I know what you are thinking when you think 'robe.' You are probably either thinking of the crushed velvet Merlin-style robe or the cushiony towel-like bathrobe. Neither is what you are looking for. You want a Wiccan-style robe. They are generally made of silk or satin and are dark purple or black. You want to have some ceremonial robes because they show that you are willing to respect the religion and make yourself look presentable when you are performing a ritual. They are also a lot less restricting than everyday clothes and allow you to move throughout your circle with ease. Of course, you should wear loose clothing underneath them, but the whole idea is to be free and able to move about with ease and grace.

Cloaks

Along with your robes, you should have a ritual cloak. Hooded cloaks are the best, in the case of inclement weather or if someone sees you in the woods performing a ritual, as you can hide your face. This world is not too kind to those who try to do magic. They equate all magic to Satan worship, which is very stereotypical and judgmental because only a very small percent of people who perform magic are devil worshipers.

Your cloak should match your robe; it is a good idea to have a pentacle sewn into it as well. A half-moon doesn't hurt either, as the half-moon is the symbol of Mother Goddess herself, and using this symbol will appeal to her greatly.

Ritual wear is very important. It is a good idea to have all these things on hand so that when you perform the ritual, you can appeal to the deities, that they may hear your spells throughout the year. You want them to want to help you, and this is one way to show them the respect they want to see.

Tools and Ingredients for Spell Work

Parchment

This is an older, more natural style of paper, and it is getting harder and harder to find. Most of the time you must go to a Wiccan supply store or a stationary store if you can find one. Parchment is very important because when you are performing a spell that requires you to write something down, it is best to use parchment due to its being the most natural type of paper. Magic seems just to roll off this paper. Think about it, whenever you read a book that talks about magic, it has always been written on parchment using old-style pens. That is because the Wiccan traditions use the most natural things they can find. If you can make a quill out of a bird feather that is the best pen there is. Parchment is just one of those things that make the spell that much better because it is natural. You do not have to use it; it is just a little helper to boost the strength of the spell.

Candles

Candles are another important part of magic. They represent fire and can bring about magic themselves, depending on their color. If you are using candles, you should choose the style and shape based on what you want to do and if you want it to burn all the way down. Candles can serve many purposes in the magical world. They can be messengers to the spirit world when you burn a wish on a piece of paper. They can use their smoke to carry your magic to where it needs to go. They can represent one of the most volatile elements there is, and they can be used for light and warmth. Candles are a necessity in your witch's pantry. Make sure you have several kinds, styles, and colors. However, make sure they are not scented because the scent can mess with the magic.

Crystals, Incense, Herbs, and Other Spellbinders

Spellbinders are important, and pretty much every spell calls for at least one of them. Often, a spell will call for multiple spellbinders, which is a great thing because one is good, two are great, and three create a spell that can't be beaten. Any more than three is overkill, though, as they will begin to drown each other out, essentially making each one ineffective. You want effectiveness; otherwise, you will not have much luck with your spells. So, remember, more than three spellbinders is overkill.

Why You Need a Book

You do not need a book per se, but if you do not keep one and you leave personal spells lying around unprotected, you can open your life to a world of trouble. If you are just a magic dabbler, you should be fine finding generic spells and writing them down so that you can use them. However, if you plan on really immersing yourself in this culture, you must create some personal spells.

That is where a book of shadows comes in. It protects your personal spells and protects your life from chaos. You want to make sure that you are not letting your personal life get into the hands of something or someone who will try to destroy it. The book gives you a sanctified place to keep your spells, your thoughts on magic, and observations you have made in the magic world.

You also need a book if you want to join a coven, and even most circles require that you have a book. The reason is quite simple: organization. Covens often have synchronized books for meetings and then personal shadow books for their home use, but both are extremely organized so that people can easily find what they need.

A book of shadows is almost like a rite of passage for a Wiccan. Even though you do not absolutely need one, it is a good idea to get one, even if it simply means that you feel more at home with magic and makes you feel like you are one with the magical world.

Additional Options

Of course, there are other tools that are generally optional; most of the time they don't have a huge effect on the magic woven in your spell. They are merely decorative and make you feel more at home with magic. However, some spells do call for them, and in these spells, they DO affect the magic, so you should have them on hand in case you need them. This way, you can ensure that you are prepared for the spell and that you do not miss your opening in case it is time sensitive.

Broom

The broom is a symbol of strength in the Wiccan religion. Contrary to media portrayal, it is not something you can fly on. The broom is merely a decorative item, but sometimes you need it to "sweep" negative energy – or other magical energies you do not want interfering with your magic – out of your spell.

A witch's broom is wooden and has straw at its head. You do not want to use a store-bought broom, as it will not have any magical energy due to its being processed. You will want to make your own or if you must buy one, get one from a Wiccan supply store, as their brooms are handmade and will have the energy you need.

If you decide to make your own, be sure that you sand down the handle because splinters are not a fun thing to deal with and you do not want to have any distractions when you are performing a spell. Splinters can prove to be a very big distraction, one that can throw off the balance of your magic.

Witch's Bell

Also known as a devil driver, this is a little decorative bell that wards off evil spirits in the magical realm. They were a big thing at the beginning of the Wiccan religion, but now they are not used very much, as most Wiccans do not believe that the devil exists. This is a big problem because it can lead these Wiccans to get too cocky with their magic and not use protective measures. The devil is real. He is not a little red man with a pointy tail and a pitchfork, but he is real, and he will try to mess with the purity of your magic and bring you to the dark side. A witch's bell should be rung seven times before you start your spell. This should be done in a circle around your circle to provide an extra layer of protection. Make sure you are not too hurried when you do this. You must let each strike of the bell resonate until it dies out before you move to the next position and ring the bell again.

Pentacle Slab

The pentacle slab is exactly what its name describes. It is a slab of a material with a pentagram engraved on it. Wood and stone are the most common materials, and they are very useful. The pentacle slab is used for protection of your spell, to make sure your spell goes where it is supposed to go and does not get in the hands of the wrong entity once it leaves your circle. You do not need a pentacle slab, but if you are a beginner in the magical world or are dabbling in gray magic, it is best to use this.

Mortar and Pestle

This is an important thing to have because you want to be able to grind your herbs so that you make them into poultices and do other things with them. Every witch should have a few different sizes on hand and use them regularly.

Hand Drum or Music

Rhythmic music is a good thing to have when you are performing a ritual because it gives you a steady beat to follow when you move around the circle. The more rhythmic you are, the more grace you will show, and the more smoothly your magic will litigate itself upon the world. You want to use smooth movements when working a spell because you want your spell to go smoothly.

Empty Bottles and Jars

These are important because you will need them for various things, such as witch jars and making essential oils for your spells. You want to have several on hand so that you will have them when you need them. Garage sales are a good place to find them; just make sure you wash them out well.

Long Matches

Matches are an important thing to have in your ritual. You want long ones so that you can light a candle in a dish without worrying about burning yourself. You also want long matches because most of the time you should not move your candle from its position to light it; long fireplace matches give you the reach you need to light the candle without having to pick it up and move it.

You can use a barbecue lighter if you are not able to find fireplace matches, but a match is a more natural way to light the candle and does not emit any gas that will throw off the balance of your spell. You want a good balance when you do magic, so if you can get them, fireplace matches are the way to go. You can find them at your local supermarket.

Writing Utensil

Many spells require you to write something on a piece of paper and to do something with the paper. You can use either a pen or a pencil. They both work well, but if you are using a pen, it is best to use a fountain pen and an inkwell to be more traditional and really get the effect and energy you want from your spell. Be careful, though, because if you must write something down without lifting the writing utensil, you must make sure you have enough ink in the pen.

A pencil works well if you are going to be burning the paper immediately, or if you will not need it weeks down the road, as pencil fades quickly. However, for a spell in which you need to write your wish and then burn it or put it in a witch's jar, a pencil is the best way to go because it is wood and wood is natural. Even the graphite in the pencil is a composite of natural materials. If you haven't guessed by now, natural is the best way to go with magic because natural materials come from the earth and the use of them pleases the Great Mother, Gaea. Make sure that when you choose a pencil, you go with a number one or a number two, as anything over that contains too much graphite and cancels out the natural wood effect. Even though graphite is a composite of natural materials, it is a processed material, and too much of it can throw your spell out of balance.

Baskets

Baskets are used for a lot of reasons in the Wiccan religion. They carry supplies and hold pieces of the ritual. There are many styles of baskets you can use for different types of rituals. You must make sure you are using a basket that is the right size for the ritual you are performing. Baskets can be bought at the store if they are woven, but it is better if you make a basket yourself, weaving it out of natural materials.

To weave a basket, find materials of the same length (bark works the best); do a cross hatch weave for the basket and let it curl up on itself. Pull the weave tighter until it forms a bowl. You now have a basic basket. There are many basket tutorials you can find online.

You want to have a few different styles of baskets on hand for

95

your rituals. They are not super important in the way of rituals, but some rituals call for them, and it is better to have them on hand than to find you short a basket.

Bucket of Water

A bucket of water is often used to cleanse your tools and your area before you perform your spell. It is always good to have a bucket of water on hand even if the spell does not call for it. You'll need one to clean any tool that falls on the ground so that it remains consecrated.

A bucket of water also keeps clean energy in your spell. You must make sure that your energy is clean, and when you use water, you help keep demons at bay. You can also make sure that your spell falls in the right hands of the right deity.

You want to make sure that you have a bucket of water and that you place it in your circle, not outside the circle. If you use the bucket of water correctly, it will significantly assist your spell. Let it assist your spell even if the spell does not call for it.

Ritual Wear

There are several things you should have on hand to wear for the rituals you will have to perform. You do not have to wear these for every spell, but you must have them on hand because when you are performing a true ritual, you should wear them as a sign of respect.

Rituals are performed most often on the solstices and at other times mentioned on the wheel of the year. These celebrations are very important in the Wiccan traditions; if you want to be part of the religion, it is best to make sure you observe them well. You do not want to ignore them, as they are part of a tradition. In the Wiccan religion, tradition is important, and you should try to keep it up. The beauty of Wicca is that you get to choose, but it can upset the deities if you approach this religion with a blasé attitude. You do not want to offend the deities if you want your spells to work because they are the ones that make the magic happen. You want them to want to help you, and you want them to answer your calls with eagerness. If you respect them and the traditions, they will respond to you with excitement to help.

Rituals are all different, and everyone performs his or her rituals a little differently. What ties them all together are the types of spells and the attire you wear while performing them. You want to wear the right attire because it shows that you respect the ritual and that you are willing to go the extra mile to show the deities that you mean business, that you are not just dabbling in magic for fun. This may seem like a good hobby, but it is a religion. Granted, it is a little bit more relaxed of a religion than you may be used to, but there are still expectations, and the more you follow them, the more the deities will recognize you and respect you. It is all about respect in the magical realm. You must respect the world; in return, the world will respect you.

Chapter 8: Meditation and Dreams

The purpose of learning to be a witch is to enhance your life. You can do this with magic. You can find yourself entirely engulfed in a new and more adventurous lifestyle. Enhancing your life with magic takes a lot of practice.

Magic is not something that comes easily to most people. It takes getting out of your head to achieve anything. Life enhancement is a big part of the Wiccan culture, and that is what draws a lot of people to it. However, despite a lot of people being drawn to this religion, there are a lot of people that leave it as well, and that is because they are not willing to put in the effort when it comes to enhancing their lives. They expect just to say a few phrases and the magic happens. This is due in part to how the media portrays magic. Look at the popular television series Charmed. It shows three witches, who fight evil, and all they do is use a few simple spells, and that is not reality. The same goes for most literature out there. Wiccans are portrayed as people who get together in the woods, say a few spells, wave a few herb sticks, and boom—magic. It is harder than these portrayals.

Spells take practice and require executing multiple times to master results. There are also several different parts to spells that you must master, once mastered; you get to move on to the next level and practice those spells for hours on end before you get any results. To become a powerful witch, you must put in a lot of time and be dedicated to your craft. The cost of being lazy will have you remain at the same level for ages.

You cannot expect life enhancement to make your life one of

leisure. This is yet another reason people leave Wicca. They expect to be able to make their crush fall in love with them and to use magic to become rich, and that just doesn't happen—at least not right away. Those things take hard work and dedication.

People have also joined and fell off the wagon, by becoming black witches. They found out ways to make them rich, and force someone to fall in love with them. However, that magic comes at a price, and the price is not cheap. These people will literally sell their souls to a demon to achieve what they want. You want to stay away from these witches. If one were to die from a black witch, their soul would be tortured for all eternity. You will not be reincarnated; you will be sent straight to purgatory. Purgatory is where the spirits of people who have done evil things and used black magic go to in the afterlife. It is not where you want to end up. Your spirit will be torn to pieces every day until the end of time, and even though your body will be dead, you will still be alive to feel it because you are your spirit. Let those who join Wicca and turn to black witches' parish on their own accord.

Anyways, how do you enhance your life with magic? You connect with the earth. You connect with other people. You fill your life with things that will enrich you and bring you joy. These things are possible with magic. It may seem that magic can't do anything that you can't do yourself, and maybe there may be some truth to that. However, being in the Wiccan religion, it makes it a lot easier to do these things with magic, rather than without magic.

Here's how magic can help you enhance your life:

Making Friends - Friends are hard to come by, and even if you have a big group of friends, they may not be the best of friends to have. As humans, we are attracted to what are known as shiny people. These are usually the people that are fun to hang out with. However, these shiny people are generally not the best people to be around, as they seem only to hang around if you can do something for them. Humans are also easily drawn in by dramatic people. These people are the ones that are always loud and always doing something that they shouldn't be doing. It is exciting, and it is fun. However, if they turn on you, it can be an unpleasant experience. These people can be toxic, and toxicity is the best way to ruin a friendship. You want to hang onto these people because you think that they bring a lot of joy to your life, but the truth is they are only dragging you down. Usually, people feel obligated at the requests of shiny people—starting to ring any bells? To spot a toxic friend all you should do is try to do something that you want to do for yourself or ask for a favor, and watch them try to drag you down or not participate.

This is where magic comes in. Magic will draw in the right type of friends so that you can make a lasting bond with them, and not have to worry about them walking out of your life because you reach a milestone in your life, and can't take them to the mall twenty times a week anymore. Instead, these friends will root for you, encourage you to be the best that you can be, and they will not bat an eye when you do something to improve your life.

100

WICCA BOOK OF SPELLS

Magic will help you find the love of your life and someone who will bring you soup when you are sick. You will attract the type of person who doesn't care if you are wearing your pajamas all day or wearing a $300 dress when you see them. These friends are hard to come by, and magic will fill your life with these friends. This way you can ensure that you are making friends with the right kind of people.

Help You Find True Love - True love is the hardest to find. You may fall in love several times in your life, and you may even get married, but chances are it is not everlasting love. Love is everywhere, and at times can be easy to find. However, the true love hard to find, because they are not looking for the right identifiers. They want excitement and butterflies forever, and while those are all well and good to have with your partner twenty years from now, the butterflies eventually fade, or they will not happen as frequently. When that happens, you want to still be able to wake up and kiss the person beside you good morning and feel good about it. If you don't, how will you ever love them for the rest of your life? Find someone who even when the butterflies fade, gives you a warm feeling in your heart, and makes you happy. True love is the love where you can argue all day, and then laugh and be happy for months on end. True love is waking up next to the one you love, and seeing them in their most vulnerable state, and loving them even more. This love is the love that people strive for endlessly, and it is a love that not a lot of people find. Some are tricked into thinking they found it because the butterflies last longer than usual, then they get married, and five years later, they get a divorce. This is because they just found someone that they lusted after longer than usual.

101

Enter magic. Magic will bring you someone who can make your heart race, and make you feel calm at the same time. It will bring you the person who will hold your hair when you are sick, and rub your feet when they are sore. It will bring you, someone, who will help with the dishes for the rest of your life. Someone who gets up with you at two in the morning to bake cookies when you can't sleep.

You want someone who is encouraging of the Wiccan religion so that you can be yourself around them. Once you let go and let fate show you who you should truly be with, these spells will help take your relationships, and make them strong, and at the same time help you form a bond with someone to create an unbreakable relationship. Letting fate take over is the hardest part. You want to find someone who you like, but most people do not trust fate to make that choice because they already have someone in mind to be their forever love. They do not want to relinquish that control for fear of something going away. Are you going to fall in love with someone who is truly the one for you, or are you going to spend the rest of your life fighting with the person you married, and using countless spells to try to fix your relationship? The choice is for you alone, but with a little patience, and a little time, you will find the person that you have truly been waiting for.

Courage - If you are a person who is not particularly courageous in any aspect of life, do not fret. You are not alone. The average person has at least one area in their life where they lack in the courage department. This can range from being talking to strangers, or trying to make it up in the business ladder. There are many parts of life that require

102

courage; it is impossible to be courageous enough for all of them on your own. For instance, you may be able to go skydiving, but the thought of talking to that gorgeous person who has caught your eye completely terrifies you. And that is okay because you can't be courageous at everything. Or maybe you are great at talking to people, and doing public speaking, but you are terrified to ride an elevator. There are different fears out there, and you cannot conquer your fears without courage. A lot of people overlook magic and how it can boost your courage levels up. Courage is important, and spells can make you a little stronger. As a witch, it is one of the most important things you can have because you are going to have to stand up to people. Whether it is to save an old tree from a company that wants to tear it down, or stopping a black witch from ruining someone's life, lots of acts require courage.

Magic can help, and it can bring you so much more than a little bit of courage. Magic can make you feel like you can take on the world. You will feel like you can do anything, and that is what you want. Just remember that the effects are not permanent, and you may have to reapply the spell a couple of times. Magic gives you the courage until you find it on your own, after a few times of realizing how great it feels to stand up to something that terrifies you; you will not need the spell anymore because you will be able to be courageous on you own.

Luck - Luck is hard to come by, and lots of people need it. You need luck when you are playing the lottery, and you need luck when you ask the love of your life to marry you, and that is something that not a lot of people think of either. Just like courage, luck is something that you need to get by in life. It is not always hard work that you should rely on because sometimes, hard work can only get you so far. Such as in a big law firm, where you and the partner's pet are vying for a promotion. You may do the harder jobs, and work the hardest, but they have the advantage on you because they are a favorite. In this case, a little luck may help. Luck can ensure that they are paying attention to your hard work, rather than having a clear winner picked out before the race even begins.

You can use a few simple spells to make talismans and good luck charms, as well as just cover yourself in an aura of good luck with some spells; these spells are generally not difficult. However, the more luck you desire, the stronger the witch you would have to be, because, the stronger the witch, the more powerful the spell. You also have to "reapply" less when you are more powerful. Even more, reason to practice, right? Everyone wants to be lucky, so make sure to work on becoming the best witch that you can be.

A real-life scenario would be a job interview. You want to use these spells without abandon, because the more luck you have, the better off you will be in an interview, and you will hopefully land the job with ease. Don't get too cocky, even though you may apply and interview, if you are not a good fit, you may not get the job no matter how much magic you use.

Recall there is a major difference between confidence and being cocky. Confidence knows you can do the job. Being cocky is thinking that without any training you can do it better than everyone else. Cocky is thinking that you are a shoe-in for a job you have never had any experience with. Confidence knows that you are a strong and quick learner and will be good at the job without any training. You want to be confident, yet humble. Know that you are not the perfect person for the job, but also know that you are the best candidate.

Clarity of Mind - Have you ever had a question that is burning in your mind or a decision that you had to make that was really hard? Did it take you longer than you care to admit to achieve what you wanted with these scenarios? That happens to everyone at some point in their life, and it is entirely normal. You want to have a clear mind, and it is harder to achieve than you would think. And, even if you clear your mind, a lot of times it is still hard to find a clear answer. You search and search, but there are pros and cons to everything. This makes it hard to find yourself the time to do what you want to do when you want to do it because you are still agonizing over making the decision or trying to figure everything out—decisions can be messy.

If you are having trouble figuring out where to go in life, you can use a spell to help you figure things out. There are many spells that help you open your mind to make the right decision, and a lot of it has to do with Divination. Yes, prophesying helps you make the right choices because you will be able to get an idea of what will be the outcome of your choice. There are spells out there to clear your mind, and there are spells to get the answers that you desire. These spells are the ones that you want to use to find your way in life and really make the right choices. Perhaps you are wondering if your spouse is cheating, and you do not know if you should pursue the matter. Do a spell and get the answers you are looking for. Don't feel guilty if they are not cheating. You are not going through their personal effects, rather doing your research before confronting them and that is what a rational person does.

Banishing Evil - Let's face it, a lot of times, we are surrounded by evil. This world is a demonic playground, no doubt about it. In these times, it becomes harder to find a pure environment, and a lot of times those who are good are under attack from the world. Have you ever felt like the entire world was against you, and even though the evil people seem to be living good lives, you are miserable? That is what a lot of people deal with when they try to lead decent lives because it seems that life does not want good in it and rewards evil. There are ways to keep yourself pure and keep your environment pure as well. Have a good place to do your magic. You want your mind to be pure and clean from attacks of other, evil witches as well.

There are several spells out there for purifying not only the area but your mind as well. One of the most common spell types for purification is known as smudging.

If you are practicing regularly, you should probably smudge your area before each spell, but if you are not practicing often, once a week or biweekly should suffice. Just make sure that you purify it before you do a spell. The purer you keep it, the more effect your spells will have on your life and evil forces will not be able to counteract your spells. There are several other spells that you can use to make sure that you are keeping your mind and environment pure from the evil that lurks around. Candles are essential to this (white candles especially). They give you a pure energy in which to perform your spells with. White candles act as a channel directly to the Goddess herself to help you keep other entities from answering your calls. Although most spells do not call for white candles, it is best to light one whenever you do a spell.

Healing - As you a Wicca beginner, you can relieve side effects and many other issues that dwell under and on top of the surface of one's skin. Mental illnesses are something that you can help with. While you cannot cure these diseases, you can help alleviate the symptoms of things such as depression and anxiety. You can also help someone who has PTSD sleep better at night. Magic when used to help people, including yourself, is wonderful. It also does not take a lot of magical strength to help alleviate the symptoms of illnesses, unlike with pain and suffering from a major physical injury.

Prosperity - Have you ever been unemployed and found yourself searching high and low for any source of income just to keep the lights on? It isn't fun, and nowadays it is getting harder to find jobs that are enough to pay the bills and keep food on the table. That is the downside of the world we live in. Jobs are becoming electronic and outsourced. And unfortunately, unless you live in a commune, you must have money to survive.

There are a lot of spells to help you have the upper hand with prosperity. It is a good idea to find a plethora of them to douse yourself with luck and prosperity if you are ever in need of it. The same goes with healing spells.

Chapter 9: Herbalism

Herbalism is a very common and core part of paganism. It was used way back before paganism was even thought of. Herbs are a part of our everyday lives, as we use them to season our food, and add color to our plates, but did you know that herbs used to be all that was available as medicine? It's true. Back before modern medicine came into play, herbs were used to cure ailments. Well, that and bloodletting. Which is another common practice in magic rituals? Which makes me wonder why on earth they burned witches in the 19th century when all they were doing was killing their doctors (hmm...)? Anyways, back on topic, herbalism was adapted by the Wiccan religion and is used in a lot of spells. These spells range from luck spells to health and well-being spells. There is an herb that can do pretty much anything you need it to in a spell.

Herbs are used in smudge sticks, ritual baths, spells, and witch jars. They are a very important part of the Wiccan rituals, and chances are, in most spells, you will need to use at least one type of herb, or herb oil. There are so many things that herbs can be used for it is mind boggling. Most people don't give a second thought to the basil they are putting in their stew. They never even wonder what protective magic it is bestowing on them.

There are many people who used herbs in a variety of ways. These people existed before Wiccans and still, exist today. There are so many religions out there, and a majority of them use herbs in some manner.

History of Herbalism

There are many different accounts of not only humans but animals with cognitive functioning using herbs to cure ailments. The Tanzanian chimp cures worms with the pith of the Veronian plant. Humans of the area do so as well. So humans are not the only ones who are known to use herbalism. Cats eat grass to settle their stomachs if they have indigestion. The type of grass they eat depends on the area they live in, and what's available.

Now on to the human history of herbalism. Humans have used herbalism since there were humans on the planet. Back when the cavemen roamed the earth, herbs were all they had to cure the ailments that they had. If they chose the wrong one, that could be disastrous. Since the beginning of time, people have relied on herbs for cures for sicknesses. It wasn't until the last hundred years that we really got into modern medicine.

There are even documentations that go back over fifty thousand years that show that people back then used herbs to cure sicknesses that arose over time. A lot of the herbs that they used then, we use today, though most of them are called by a different name, as plant names have changed over the season. Herbs are documented to have eased the passing of some people who were too far gone to save. And have even been known to stop the spread of yellow fever, if caught soon enough. Herbs were there throughout bouts of epidemics, the bubonic plague, the red death, so many other diseases have been combated by herbs until modern medicine came along and completely knocked them out.

Shamanism and the Early Herbal Pioneers

Back before you were even thought of. Before your mother was even thought of, well, even before your grandmother was even thought of there were shamans and herbal pioneers. These people were in charge of taking care of the sick in a village and blessing young mothers, and anything else that needed herbal magic. These people were often revered, but in some cultures they were outcast. It all depends on if Roman Catholicism had made it to the area then.

There are many shamans in the world, and contrary to popular beliefs, they don't all live in the mountains of Indonesia. There are many in the United States, even in New York. Shamans are everywhere in the world, and they still are in practice today. They use herbs to tell your future, to heal you spiritually, and physically. They use herbs for so many things, and it is astounding how many ways they can help with nothing but what they find in the earth.

Shamans are always depicted as an old man who lives at the top of a mountain, but the truth is there are more Native American shamans than there are Indonesian shamans. It is actually a common practice for the natives to call upon their shamans, known as medicine men, to heal them. Some tribes still do not go to hospitals unless absolutely necessary. They choose to trust their own people, with good reason, but we are not going to get into politics in this book.

Medicine men are often tribe elders or a member of the elder's family. Sometimes the medicine men are actually women, but they are generally men, as women are seen as needed to take care of the children and the dwelling, and to cook for the men when they bring home the meat.

In Egypt, they were known to use herbalism to cure people and poison them. Herbalism was rampant in ancient Egypt, even being used as the first embalming techniques. These techniques were used to help keep the bodies preserved as well as possible because they believed that a decaying body was an invitation for the devil to steal the soul. So they made an archaic version of formaldehyde with plants that they found available to them.

Herbalism was used heavily in Saudi Arabia and still is today. There are many people in ancient history and history today that use herbs for medicinal purposes, and not for just food.

Magic and Medicine

There is a lot of magic in the world. A lot of it is found in older style medicine. In the olden days, medicine was based on a lot of pagan magic. Medicine and magic have known to go hand in hand so much so, that a lot of really religious Catholics refused to see a doctor when they were sick, and would rather die than be touched by "wicked magic." A lot of them did die due to the complications and issues from their ailments.

Medicine was very different than it is today, as there were no pills. Whiskey and rum were prescribed as cough syrup, and marijuana was prescribed for aches and pains regularly. Basic herbs today were mixed up for potions, tonics, and poultices. While there was not always a spell said over the herbs, a lot of the tonics and potions were a lot like magic rituals done by shamans.

111

Many Meanings of Herb

There are many different meanings of the word herb. With so many different cultures out there, it makes sense that the translation may be a little different from group to group. Some groups are more closed on the meaning, and some are more open, it all depends on what is available in their area.

Herbs in Practice

Herbs are an essential part of the Wiccan culture, as a lot of spells depend on a variety of herbs to be successful. Smudges are another thing that relies on herbs. In fact, smudge sticks are made up entirely of herbs. You take the herbs, roll them into a bundle, and then you light them and use the smoke to cleanse the area.

You can use oils on the object you wish to bless, or you can use it to anoint the candle you are using to do the ritual.

Flowers are very common as well. A Wiccan may use a combination of all three (herb, oils, flowers) in a spell as well. There is no limit to what you can do when you combine herbs.

You can use herbs in your everyday life as well, in common foods, and choose the herbs that you need for your day. Herbs are very helpful in your food, and in your drinks to go on with your day. They mesh well with the human body and lifestyle.

Including Oils

This is something that very few groups do. Wiccans are a part of the select few. Oils can help in many different spells and healing balms. These groups find things such as castor oil and coconut oil useful. There are many other oils that are an essential part of the Wiccan culture as well.

Including Flowers

Some groups include flowers as herbs. Apple blossoms, chamomile, and carnation flowers are often used. Rose petals are used in a lot of Wiccan spells. Flowers can be just as useful as the green leafy plants that most people associate herbs with. You can use almost every type of flower out there for some part of a ritual.

Only Grass & Branch Like

Some people only count the leafy plants as herbs. These are what a lot of people consider herbs. Thyme, basil, beech, thistle, and other branch like, leafy, green plants are classified as herbs.

Magical Power of Plants

Intelligent Life on Earth

Humans are not the only form of intelligent life on earth. In fact, every species is intelligent in their own way. Just because they do not have the same reasoning skills as us, doesn't mean that they are not intelligent, and do not have their own hierarchy of cognitive skills. If they didn't, all dogs would have the same learning abilities, but as you will find, some dogs are smarter than others.

Herbs help the intelligent life on earth. Herbs help even the least responsive of intelligent creatures. They often use them for indigestion or other problems that bother them. Chimpanzees seem the most knowledgeable about herbs, using herbs for everything from worm reduction and cures to spreading banana on injuries to help speed up the healing process.

Plants themselves are considered intelligent life by some, as they feel what goes on around them. A tree actually feels pain, and a polygraph test can register the pain. That is how herbs work. They send their energy out into the atmosphere around you, and you use their energy to send a message out into the world to do what you need them to.

The Power of Correspondence

This is not the type of correspondence you would see between friends. You don't write letters to your herbs. Herbal correspondence is literally how the herb talks to the world. Herbal correspondences refer to the workings of the herb, and how it reacts to the world around it (and other herbs).

Herbal correspondence is a very powerful thing, as it can literally change your entire day, and can make or break a spell. Knowing the correspondences will help you figure out if a spell is for protection, or if it is for wealth. It will also keep you from turning a spell about power into a humbling spell.

You want to know the correspondences of each herb that you work with, and some essential herbs will be listed in a later section for you to learn a little more about.

Getting Acquainted with Herbs

We all have to start somewhere, so if you know nothing or very little about herbs, then you is at the right place. This section is going to cover the basics t about the main herbs that are used in Wiccan traditions. You will learn what they do and how to use them.

After you bind up the smudge stick, you have to dry it if the

WICCA BOOK OF SPELLS

herbs are not already dry. To dry it, wrap it in paper, and change the paper every day for ten days. In ten days' time, you will have a dry smudge stick.

Basil

Basil is an herb that you often find in your local supermarket. It is a very strong, natural tasting herb that almost has a little bit of spice to it. It is green and leafy like. This herb gives you protection of the spirit. It is also used in a lot of home protection spells as well. It brings wealth while repelling negativity and it is a sacred plant.

You want this plant in your home. It will bring you peace of mind knowing that its mystical powers are watching over you. Try making a smudge stick combined with some other herbs such as sage, and smudging your house with it to ward off any evil that may be lurking, and creating a protective shield over your household.

Basil is one of the most used herbs in spells due to its versatility. It is essential that you have a stock of it both crushed and full in your store room, and maybe keep a little around for quick access.

Chamomile

Chamomile is an herb that is very easily found. It is often used as a tea leaf and makes a very delicious cup of hot tea. It is very sweet, with just an air of bitterness on the back of the tongue. This combination of such starkly contrasting flavors is what makes it so desirable for people to drink. But this herb is more than just good for the popular beverage; it has other purposes as well.

It is great for meditation. It soothes the inner soul and keeps you grounded to the earth while you meditate. It pushes all of your inner troubling's away and calms you mentally and spiritually. This allows you to balance out your mind before you meditate. Try drinking a cup of chamomile tea with Valerian root sweetened with a little honey before your next meditation session.

This herb also attracts money and is often used in prosperity charms. When used in the right spells, it can attract a small amount of wealth to you, and when coupled with other wealth attractants, can attract even more wealth to you.

Chamomile is a great herb and is an easy one to use if you do not want to cast a circle and make a smudge stick. Just make a cup of tea, say your piece over it, and drink it.

Cinnamon

I am pretty sure everyone in the universe knows this beautiful and flavorful spicy stick. It is a holiday season must have for people of the Christian religion, but for Wiccans, it is so much more. This little doodad is a triple threat in the pantry if you know what I'm saying.

That's right. It is an aphrodisiac. It can draw someone close to you and is charged with romantic energy. And not just the hold your hand on a Saturday night type of romance. The whole nine yards romance. The type that people will be begging for more of.

But not only is it an aphrodisiac, it is also used to draw power and success to you. Use this in a spell about domination in the work place, and you might just achieve it if you have enough.

This small brown roll of energy is just what you need in your pantry to get life going the way you want it to be.

Dandelion

Dandelion, the tiny yellow plant that as it develops turns into nothing but fluffy white seeds. These little plants are mysterious in how they work. They start out beautiful, and then they turn into these cute white little puff balls that remind you of a bunny's tail, and if you blow on that puffball it spreads hundreds of seeds everywhere, and you make a wish for those seeds to carry away. At least that is what we are taught as children anyway.

In reality, dandelions don't grant wishes. They do, however, bring inner peace. You may find that your spirit calms when you blow on a dandelion and you may even feel energized. That's because those are two of the main properties of this herb. As you blow on the dandelion, you are releasing its correspondences into the air.

Dandelions also enhance your prophetic powers. They do this through your dreams. Try putting a vase of them beside your bed (preferably while they are in the flowering phase, otherwise, you may have a mess.) When you go to bed, stare at the dandelions until you fall asleep. In the morning write down your dreams, and look for a pattern. You may have been blessed with a prophecy.

Elecampane

This herb is known for its healing properties. It is a root herb that is often used to clear up bronchial infections, but it has a lot of other wonderful well-being aspects to it as well.

It is great for protecting you from getting pneumonia, and it is used to strengthen the immune system. While it is not used for much outside the realm of protection, it is very important to have if you want to do a healing spell.

Hibiscus

Hibiscus is the beautiful flower that is commonly found in Hawaii. It is the cousin of the Lotus flower and is quite gorgeous. The flower is known for its use in leis and other jewelry that Hawaiians wear, and it is just all around a good flower.

The hibiscus flower is known to attract love and lust to those who wear it or its scent. If you are looking for a powerful love spell, this is the one to attract your one true love. Be careful, though, if not done correctly, you will only attract a lot of lustful lovers, and if that is not what you are looking for, it can make it harder to find your true love.

If you are into divination, this plant will also help you, as it can help open your third eye to the future. You need only to trust it. It will also help with dreams like the dandelion. Try combining them for some powerful visions in your dreams.

Lavender

This purple flower is very important in a witch's stock. It has several uses, but most of them all have to do with its soothing aroma. Admit it, lavender anything smells pretty nice, as long as they use pure lavender oil, and not a synthetic lavender scent that is headache inducing, sickly sweet, and honestly makes it smell like you have a gas leak in your house.

Lavender is a purifying herb. This means it's used to banish any bad things that are in your house, life, or anywhere else. It is like the cleaning agent of the herb world. It will cleanse you from head to toe and leave you feeling fresh as if you had just taken a shower.

It is also used for giving you sweet dreams. There are bath lotions out there for adults and babies alike that are for this exact purpose. You use them before you go to bed right after your bath or shower, and you will sleep easy. It is encouraged for parents to give their babies a bath in this every night before bed to help them establish a sleep pattern.

Lavender is a great herb to keep with you pretty much at all times in a little emergency herb bag. You can use it whenever you need it.

Mugwort

This is a very spiritual herb. It is used to open the doors to your inner soul. If you are scared to see the depth of your truest self, don't use too much of this herb.

It enhances the moons psychic receptive qualities and allows

119

you to be more in tune with the world around you as well as with yourself. You can use this if you want to open your eyes to the things around you and see things for what they truly are.

Nutmeg

This is not just a topping for your hot cocoa or eggnog. This is actually a very useful herb in the Wiccan culture.

It is a great relaxation tool and can be used to ease stresses. That is why it is often used in such calming relaxing drinks. It also invites happiness into your life. So if you want to be stress-free and happy, this is the herb for you.

Rosemary

This is a very useful herb in the kitchen and our lives. Most people only see rosemary as an herb to brine a turkey in, or to brighten up a plate, but it is so much more than that.

This herb gives you clarity. It helps you see the world for what it truly is. Mixed with mugwort, it can be a powerful combination. You will see the world clearly for possibly the first time if you use these in a clarity spell.

It will also give you inner peace, so if you have something that is bugging you, and you just can't seem to let it go, then you should put some rosemary in tea, and drink it. It will help you find your inner clarity.

Sage

Sage has many uses, and a lot of times it depends on the type of sage that you are using. I know a lot of people think sage is sage, but there is sage that is almost white, sage that is purple, there is even really dark green type of sage. Sage comes in a variety of colors and has a variety of uses.

It can bring about inner peace and wisdom to boot. Inner peace is what we all strive for, and if it is mixed with rosemary, you will find yourself calm and collected so that you can gather the wisdom that you need without an inner battle raging on inside your head.

It can also aid fertility, healing, and help you lead a long and happy life. If that sentence right there is not enough for you to put sage on everything in your life, I don't know what is. Sage is the master of life, death, and everything in between it seems.

Sage can also be used for cleansing, purification, and protection. I mean, is there anything it can't do? Other than making your crush fall in love with you, I don't believe there is anything else that it can't do.

Thyme

This is the butt of many people's holiday jokes due to how the name is pronounced. However, this branch like herb is not just for jokes. It can improve longevity in your life, and make you stronger and have more energy. With the energy to get stuff done, and the life left to do it in, you may find you have a little extra thyme on your hands (sorry, couldn't resist).

It's a great confidence booster. It can help you get the courage to talk to the guy or girl that you are crushing on, or give you the courage to go for that big promotion. This is just all around a great herb to have in your stock.

Astrology and the Elements in Gardening

Unlike with normal gardening, the elements and astrology have a lot to do with herbal gardening, because they are what infuse the herbs with their magical properties. Just like humans have astrological signs, so do plants. And some are best planted at different times and picked at different times. You must learn when to plant a certain plant to gain the most magic out of them.

Some plants only grow the best, hence with the most magic, if planted during the right moon cycle. So you have to pay close attention to when that is as well. While it takes a lot of work, you will be sure to get the most magic out of your plants if you plant them at the right times according to what they need.

Practical and Magical Tips for Working with Herbs

There are many things that you should remember when you are going to be working with herbs, as well as when you're purchasing them. Herbs only work when they are in the right conditions, and if they have been picked at the right time, or planted, at the right time.

Herbs are great in spells, but they are tricky, and they work best under the right conditions.

Creating Your Own Herb Garden

The best way to avoid being bamboozled with herbs that were not carefully cultivated is to create your own magical garden, and filling it with the herbs of your choice. Be careful, though, because herbs can be very finicky plants to grow, and you may have to try a few times before you have any success even getting them to grow, let alone getting them to grow well enough to use in your spells.

When you are planting your garden, you should take into consideration all of the things that go into growing a garden, and then the magical aspects of growing your own magical herb garden. Things such as astrology, moon cycles, timing, and much more.

Once you have got it all down, you'll find that you are saving money by growing your own herbs, and it is nice to always have a supply on hand when you need them.

Purchasing Herbs

When you are purchasing herbs already planted and picked, make sure that you are buying whole herbs, and from a place that caters to witches and the Wiccan religion (if possible) to ensure that they are planted and picked at the right time. You also don't want to buy pre-crushed herbs, because some spells call for you to crush them a certain way, and some spells call for the herb to be intact, and if this is the case, that means that you would then have to buy an intact herb to add to your collection. It is a lot easier to buy them whole and crush them yourself.

Also, when purchasing herbs, make sure that you purchase

most of them dry if you are just doing it for storage. If you have a ritual in a day or two that requires fresh herbs and you are already at the shop, then go ahead and buy fresh, but for most rituals, you only need dried herbs.

If you are purchasing online, only go through a trusted Wiccan provider. Otherwise, you may not get what you think you were supposed to be getting. You could get herbs that were picked at the wrong time or planted just a little too late. You want ones that are just right.

Drying and Storing Herbs

It's important that if you pick fresh herbs, you dry them right away unless you just picked them for a ritual you are doing that night that requires fresh herbs.

To do this lay the herbs out flat on a piece of paper and cover them with another piece of paper. Leave them like this for ten days, changing the paper daily. Then you should store them in a cool, dry, dark place to keep from charging them with the wrong energy.

Conclusion

In this guide, I have tried to provide an unbiased approach, though undoubtedly my own experiences as a practicing Wiccan might have influenced certain sections of this book. Generally speaking, I have tried to include the most **"popular"** approach to each topic, as this should make the information easier to digest, and you are also more likely to encounter Wiccans with the same set of beliefs—this might make it easier for you to find a local coven with a set of beliefs that truly resonate with you.

However, nothing in this inspiring, fascinating religion is set in stone. The great thing about Wicca is that you are free to come up with your own belief system, and as you meet and interact with fellow practitioners, you'll see that some people's interpretations might vary wildly from the views presented in this guide.

There is no right or wrong. As long as you keep the Wiccan principles at heart, and never intentionally seek to harm others, you can practice Wicca in any way you see fit. In fact, I would actively **encourage** you to seek out your own path.

One of the best things about Wicca is that your interpretations, views, and beliefs are highly flexible.

Over time, when you begin to embrace Wicca in your daily life, you might have certain epiphanies that re-shape your approach to the practicing this religion. What you believe on day one, might be **very** different to your beliefs on day 100, which could be a world apart from your views on day 1,000. It can be a lifelong journey, and even after decades you will still find yourself learning new things. This is one of the many benefits of keeping your own Book of Shadows—you can literally track how your Wiccan journey has evolved over time.

Remember: nobody can tell you how to practice Wicca, and the religion can mean anything you want it to mean to you. And when you read another guide to the topic, you will likely come across even more conflicting information!

That's just the way Wicca is. Even if you encounter some different opinions—even those completely opposed to what you have read in this guide!—it doesn't mean one guide is right, and another is wrong: it just means the many different authors have interpreted different aspects of the religion differently.

I will leave you with that thought, as it is now time for you to start your own journey, and interpret the information presented to you in your own way. I have included a number of tables of correspondence at the end of this guide, which you should find helpful at some point in time. I have also included a number of suggested sources for further reading, as in the early days it is important for you to absorb as much information as possible on the subject.